CW00686080

EFFECTIVE PERFORMANCE MANAGEMENT

EFFECTIVE PERFORMANCE MANAGEMENT

A Strategic Guide to Getting the Best from People

JOHN LOCKETT

First published in 1992

Kogan Page Limited
120 Pentonville Road
London N1 9JN

British Library Cataloguing in Publication Data

A CIP record for this book is available from the British Library.

ISBN 0 7494 0420 5

Typeset by Saxon Printing Ltd, Derby
Printed in England by Clays Ltd, St Ives plc.

Contents

List of Figures

List of Tables

Preface

In order to be effective, organisations need to have a clear mission and good management of performance to ensure that the mission is achieved. Similarly, writers need to have a clear idea about what they want to achieve. Writing a book is an exercise in marketing, trying to resolve an unfilled need in what has become an active market. Some writers have filled a particular niche very effectively – Meredith Belbin in team-building and Michael Porter in corporate strategy are excellent examples. There is, in my view, a need for a book which brings several of these ideas together into a coherent and comprehensive programme which an organisation can follow in order to be fully effective in the management of performance.

The concept of the performance cycle and an understanding of the supporting policies and processes which make the cycle work effectively is a way of helping managers and organisations achieve their mission by good performance management. Management of Performance is *the* key task for organisations and individuals today; a critical factor if the organisation is to compete in today's turbulent market place.

It is appropriate here to acknowledge my debt to some of the writers and thinkers whose work has influenced my approach to performance management – Charles Handy's work on future organisation structures, Tom Peters approach to managing in turbulence, Beverley Potter's work on personal career development, Honey and Mumford's learning styles and Peter Herriot's book on recruitment. My effrontery in expanding their ideas is borne of a desire to explain, to interpret and to package the vast amount of work on management science into a readable format which can be understood and implemented by busy managers in complex organisations working within competitive markets.

This is not an academic book. I am a personnel manager, recently turned consultant. My work is not derived from academic research, although I have read widely in the search for useful and practical concepts which can help organisations improve their management of performance. Rather, it is through personal experience of working with managers that I have discovered ways of improving work methods and ways in which organisations can support those efforts.

I would particularly like to thank colleagues with whom I have worked, both as a personnel manager and management consultant. Many people have helped me to formulate my ideas, but I alone take the responsibility for the way they have been set down. Over the years I have spent many hours discussing these matters with my friend and colleague Simon Standish and gratefully acknowledge his influence on the book. I would also like to thank Gill Wink for her patience and fortitude in deciphering multiple written drafts and almost incomprehensible tapes of dictation.

Finally, to my wife and children, many thanks for their tolerance of my regular disappearance into the study (normally at bath times) and for their support in the project. Managing a full consultancy workload whilst writing a book leaves less time for the family and I am grateful for their forbearance.

John Lockett, 1992

1

The Emancipation of Sisyphus

My working title for this book was 'The Emancipation of Sisyphus'. It was vetoed as a final title for very sensible reasons, but I wanted to introduce Sisyphus at an early stage because, to me, he symbolises the old style of organisation where people were paid for attendance and effort – that is, turning up and working hard without any sense of purpose in helping the organisation achieve its objectives.

Sisyphus – not a social disease but the mythological victim condemned, in Hades, to push a large stone uphill, only to see it constantly roll back down again. In *The Myth of Sisyphus* (Gallimard, 1942) Albert Camus, the French novelist, described his fate thus:

> The gods had condemned Sisyphus to ceaselessly rolling a stone to the top of a mountain, whence the stone would fall back of its own weight. **They had thought with some reason that there is no greater punishment than futile and hopeless labour.**

This book aims to bring about the emancipation of Sisyphus and others like him by reviewing how organisations can avoid putting their staff through 'futile and hopeless labour'. Sisyphus would feel at home in many organisations today. You can imagine him sitting at his desk moving paper from in-tray to out-tray, attending the occasional meeting and then starting all over again the next morning – busy, safe, bored. And stagnating.

The Sisyphus syndrome is one of misdirected effort – people working hard but, for a variety of reasons, neither performing nor developing. It could be that the organisation is structured badly so that Sisyphus is a middle manager, trapped between too many levels like a confused motorist in a multi-storey car park. Or perhaps Sisyphus has no incentive to do anything other than continue to push his rock up a hill – maybe he once suggested buying a mechanical digger to lighten his burden and received a whack round his ear for his pains. There are many reasons why people fail to perform at work and the aim of this book is to suggest ways in which performance can be enhanced and directed to support the objectives of the organisation.

MANAGING PERFORMANCE

Managing performance – and the managers within them – is the main function of organisations in today's turbulent business environment. This is a continuous process in which organisations clarify the level of performance required to meet their strategic objectives, convert them into unit and individual objectives and manage them continually in order to ensure, not only that they are being achieved but also that they remain relevant and consistent with overall strategic objectives.

There are several factors which are critical to my theme that management of performance is the only *management* function within an organisation. It is not only to manage day to day performance, but to sustain it in whatever business environment predominates. Effective performance management is the only mechanism for the effective management of change – that is, clarifying what the organisation needs to do, translating that into clear goals and reviewing those goals regularly.

There have been several changes in the business world which have created the need to manage performance more closely than before:

- In almost all sectors, competition is becoming more intense. This is true even in public sector services like the National Health Service. This puts a greater responsibility onto the managers within organisations to respond to consumer demand and ensure that these demands are met in full at a competitive price.
- This is made more difficult by the increasing tendency to segmentation of markets into small, *niche* markets. Niche markets are like small harbours; they cannot be entered by supertankers (the centralised monolithic organisations of the past). The only way that supertankers can gain access to these small harbours is to send small boats ('strategic business units') with clear objectives and a wide remit. However, the captain of the supertanker must give the landing party enough authority to respond to events when they finally make land. This is the essence of good performance management – managing the 'what', 'where' and 'when', but leaving the 'how' to the person doing the job. With greater decentralisation of organisations and a more confident and assertive workforce, this is the only way that many organisations can operate in an increasingly volatile environment.

- Reduction in management levels has also increased the need to improve the management of performance. In the old pyramidal-style organisation, managers spent much of their time in a 'post box' role, moving information from top to bottom – carrying out some broad management functions, but more often reduced to close supervision of their subordinates – supervision rather than management. With the removal of several layers of middle management, their role is beginning to change, with wider spans of control and an increase in 'working managers', ie managers who have professional functions to perform in addition to their pure management role. In the public sector, senior professionals are beginning to increase their managerial workload whilst continuing to exercise other demanding responsibilities. Thus, their management role *must* be one of clarifying what needs to be done, whilst leaving the minutiae increasingly to their staff.

There has been a shift in the philosophical approach to work, heralded by writers and thinkers like Charles Handy and Tom Peters. The shift is from effort to performance.

Sisyphus worked hard but didn't get anywhere. There used to be an heroic satisfaction in a Stakhanovite devotion to duty – but no longer. There is an urgent need for people at work to achieve results – results which meet the company's performance requirements. Scoring 'A' for effort is no longer relevant, unless that effort is harnessed towards these requirements. This applies particularly to support functions, who may, in the past, have worked long and hard in pursuit of some private or professional agenda. Their professional competence must now be focused on specific business requirements, not on some interesting but obscure aspects of their own profession.

Before moving on to look at some of the issues related to performance management, I want to clarify some of the benefits of effective performance management throughout the organisation. Performance management is not simply a new fad, it is a disciplined approach to management which should ensure that the whole organisation is committed to, and capable of, providing a quality product or service. The benefits of effective performance management should be apparent to all major stakeholders in the organisation's network.

Benefits of effective performance management

Effective performance management will benefit all of the following:

- **Top management** – it should enable them to get on with their job of setting objectives for the organisation whilst managing relationships with external bodies – customers, politicians, regulatory bodies, shareholders – and translating their requirements into objectives for the organisation.

- **Managers** – it will help them to gain a full understanding of the organisation's mission, set targets and standards for their team and delegate work, freeing them to concentrate on strategic planning and the continuous improvement and development of their operations and work team.
- **People within the organisation** – improved management of performance should result in clearer targets, and the freedom to work autonomously to achieve these targets, with the right level of support from their management, ie improved personal self-development.
- **Support functions** – objectives which come from a centrally agreed business plan are more likely to give support functions an alternative raison d'etre rather than the pursuit of their own specialised agenda. Most line/staff conflicts can be traced to a lack of shared objectives. These relationships need to be managed by a form of performance contract, so that professional competence can be focused on agreed business objectives and not dissipated on other issues.
- **Customers** – clear performance management should enable the organisation to deliver its consumer promise more consistently by converting customer needs into workable plans of action.

The whole organisation should benefit by a reduction in wasted effort, development of productive working relationships between and within functions and achievement of its business plans, both present and future.

THE ECOLOGY OF PERFORMANCE MANAGEMENT

Performance management is creeping slowly and inexorably into the vocabulary of managers and consultants, as did one of its conceptual predecessors – total quality management (TQM). TQM became, in some organisations, a powerful discipline for the effective implementation of business strategies, embracing the whole organisation. Elsewhere it became the ephemeral application of some trendy ideas which were quickly replaced by the next generation of meretricious management techniques.

Performance management can be applied in similar ways. It is represented in some organisations merely as a good appraisal system; in others it is an attempt to redirect the whole organisation towards superior performance. The limitations of traditional performance management approaches have been threefold. First, they have been identified with annual programmes of appraisal and target-setting. They have operated typically on a cascade basis with very little participation from the subordinate. Secondly, they have focused on the management of individual performance whilst taking very little account of the relationship between the individual and the organisation, except perhaps in relation to the reward structure of the organisation. Thirdly, they have not attempted to bring together the many disciplines within the management of people into a coherent and coordinated programme.

During my research and development for this book, one particularly apt metaphor recurred – the concept of performance management as *ecological* rather than as a series of unrelated functions. Essentially, ecology is the study of the relationships between living organisms and the environment in which they live. It transcends and coordinates the main scientific disciplines so that we can gain a greater range of knowledge about the interaction of organisms with each other and with the living and non-living parts of the environment in which they exist. This seems to me to be an accurate reflection of the lives of people within organisations. Performance management should consider not only the people *within* an organisation but their interaction with each other and the technical parts of their organisation.

Similarities between the ecology of nature and the ecology of organisational performance

Both nature and organisational performance deal with dynamic, and often chaotic environments. It can be helpful to regard a business organisation as an ecosystem, which responds to changes within wider ecosystems – eg local, national and global economic and political activities and changing social trends. Like any ecosystem, organisations have some relatively stable elements but they also have a profusion of complex interactions and transactions. The process of studying organisations is one of increasing complexity and the shape of this trend has been reflected by the titles of recent management best sellers such as *Thriving on Chaos* and *The Age of Unreason*.

Organisations, like ecology, deal with living organisms – people – not just systems and machines operated by hands. These people are becoming increasingly demanding and expect to be treated as individuals, not just as part of an impersonal collective. Performance managers need to take this into account and give their people scope to manage their work in their own way whilst providing direction to ensure that their performance is directed towards supporting the strategy and values of the organisation.

The concept of adaption is critical to the understanding of ecology as it is for the effective management of organisations. The survival of a species is a factor of its own genetic constitution and its ability to adapt to changes in its environment. Ecologists make the distinction between *adjustment* to the environment (small changes required by slightly changed circumstances) and a more profound *adaptability* which enables organisms to survive in a wide range of environmental circumstances. This is referred to as the concept of natural selection, or 'survival of the fittest', where 'fitness' relates to the probability of survival and growth within a range of possible environments over a period of time. The concept of organisational fitness is critical to the achievement of high performance within an organisation. High achievers cannot achieve their potential if their organisation has not fully adapted to its business environment.

Relationships between organisms in an ecosystem are as important as those between the organism and the ecosystem. The relationships in a local pond between predators and prey are mirrored within most business organisations. In effect, a business organisation is a vast internal market which mirrors the requirements of the external market – competing for scarce resources, finding appropriate niches to establish your capacity to contribute, explaining and promoting your services to your internal customer and delivering your service at the lowest cost through the most appropriate mechanism. Ecological textbooks talk about competition between species and niches almost as much as the other eco-science, economics (both words, incidentally, come from the same root). Relationships within organisations are directly relevant to performance management because without harmonious relationships and agreement on purpose and objectives, the organisation's performance is likely to be less effective.

This ecological concept of an organism existing within an ecosystem is appropriate for all issues of performance by organisations and within them. An organisation exists within the wider national and global economy; it is more likely to be profitable and successful when the economic climate is growing than when the economy is in recession. In recession, we see previously healthy organisations suddenly becoming less effective, sometimes to the extent that they go into liquidation. This is often due to a failure to anticipate or to adapt to a change in the economic climate.

Inside the organisation, similar situations prevail. If the organisation is well structured with few barriers to high performance and many incentives, the performance of individuals within it is likely to be high. If, however, the organisation has an ineffective structure, then even highly competent people are likely to be frustrated when they try to improve their performance. The difference between extra- and intra-organisational performance is that the organisation can influence its own internal structure and performance, whereas it has less control over its external environment.

To conclude the metaphorical comparison the following points should be noted:

- An organisation can enhance the performance of its staff by removing barriers and creating incentives to achieve high levels of performance.
- An organisation is an ecosystem within larger ecosystems. It must be structured in a way that enhances its ability to adapt to change within its environment. Thus, the management of organisational performance must relate to achieving today's targets to ensure survival whilst also making plans to prepare for the challenges of tomorrow.

This analogy can be examined on another level; the relationship of the individual to the organisation. People within the organisation must achieve high levels of performance today in order to ensure survival until tomorrow but, at the same time, individual capability must be increased in order to ensure that their organisation continues to survive in whatever business environment predominates; that they remain adaptable to the changing demands put on them by their organisation; and that they have the competence to achieve increasingly high levels of performance.

The relationship between performance and competence

Quite simply, an individual's measurable performance cannot exceed their competence. Lack of competence, ie applied skill and knowledge, is a barrier which may prevent people from higher performance. Self-evidently, we cannot perform as well in areas where we have little ability or potential as we can in areas where we have higher levels of skill and knowledge. Competence forms the boundary of our capacity to perform. Effective performance management should, therefore, focus on two objectives:

1. Ensuring that people are motivated to perform effectively to the boundaries of their ability
2. Stretching those boundaries by an effective programme of personal development

Performance management processes which focus only on achieving results run the risk of ignoring the development of competence and thus may achieve this year's targets at the expense of those of the next year – and next year may never come. Effective managers and effective organisations balance the need to maximise current performance with the need to develop capability for the future. Performance management, therefore, needs to apply to two concepts – *performance*, ie the achievement of agreed targets; and *competence*, the development of the skills and knowledge required to survive in the current and future business environment.

The essence of performance management is the development of individuals with competence and commitment, working towards the achievement of shared meaningful objectives within an organisation which supports and encourages that achievement. Of course, that is all very well if you say it quickly! It seems a relatively easy thing to do. The one element missing so far is one which is not available to the ecologist – a formal management structure. Organisations are managed and part of their management process is the clarification of direction for their members. This cannot, as in the ecological environment, be done by osmosis or extra-sensory perception. Structured management is the mechanism for converting organisational goals into measurable achievement.

A manager's key responsibility within an organisation is the conversion of corporate strategy, customer requirements, shareholders' needs and all the other strategic issues into achievable action plans for their team. This process goes on right across and down the organisation – it is the movement from the rarefied atmosphere of strategy into the arena of getting things done. The work group is the organisation in microcosm and the manager is to the work group what the chief executive is to the whole organisation. The work group in this context may be a division, a team, a working party, a hospital ward, a class or any other unit. The important thing is that it should be the work group for which a manager has responsibility. The manager is the funnel through which the various external and internal policies and strategies are poured and converted into action plans.

The rational process

A manager fulfils several roles:

- creating a sense of mission by clarifying what the work group is there to do;
- creating a clear organisation structure so that the work of individuals and the team as a whole can be concentrated on achieving the goals required and not dissipated into pointless administration and bureaucracy;
- clarifying the critical success factors required, and creating an appropriate mechanism to ensure continuous improvement;

- ensuring that there is continuous development of assets, structures, processes and people to achieve today's objectives and prepare to achieve those of tomorrow.

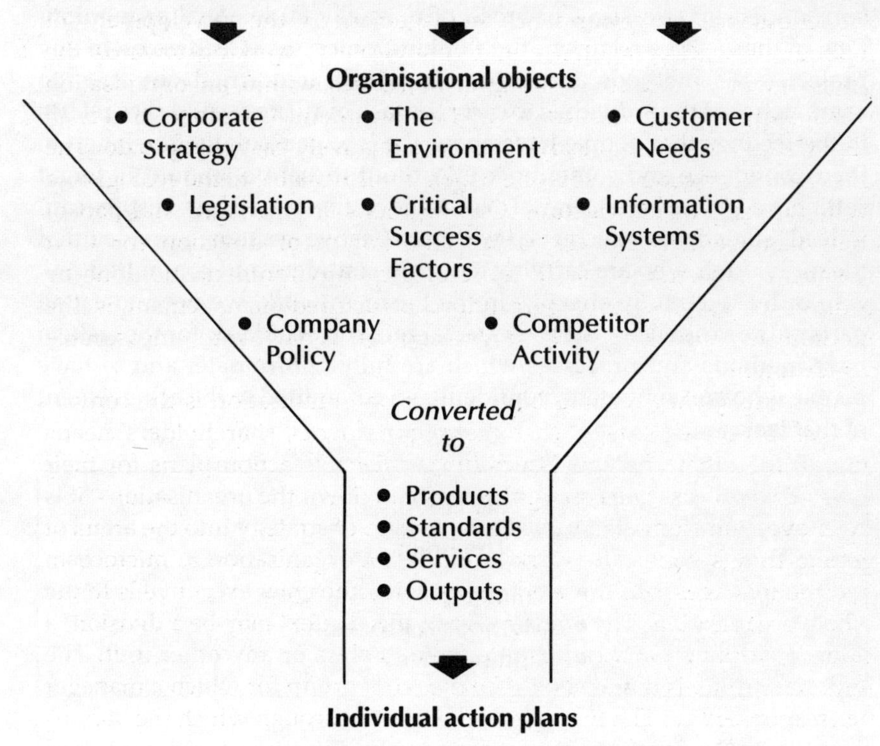

Figure 1 *The 'corporate funnel'*

The manager's role has been reframed from the old style corporate 'postman' to corporate funnel. In traditional bureaucracy, orders came down a tube to be passed further down, often undigested. Now they are 'mixed' in a funnel by the manager (see Figure 1).

THE PERFORMANCE 'SANDWICH'

The management of performance is not, as many theorists have tried to make it, an entirely logical process. In some organisations, it has been reduced to a series of systems and processes – target setting, appraisal and review. Practising managers know, however, that it is not enough to have efficient performance management systems. There is a need to engage the full enthusiasm of the individual in the achievement of their work, otherwise those systems become simply an additional bureaucratic procedure. Figure 2 illustrates the full performance management task. The task in hand is the 'meat' in the performance sandwich and it is surrounded by two slices of bread of normally fairly equal proportion. One of those slices relates to the thinking processes which go on in any project – the methods and processes which are carried out and the competence of the individual to carry the task out. The second slice relates to the feelings that people have about the job, particularly in relation to their confidence and commitment. Without these, no amount of target setting and effective appraisal will achieve the task. High results can, indeed, sometimes be achieved without effective systems, provided that the individuals who are carrying it out are confident and committed.

In order to be fully effective in the business world we need to eat all parts of the sandwich – to have clear targets and standards for the task, to have methods and processes which are fully appropriate, and to have people who are competent, confident and committed to the achievement of that task.

CEREBRAL

The Brain

- Thinking
- Methods & Processes
- Competence

THE TASK

- Targets
- Standards

VISCERAL

The Guts

- Feelings
- Confidence
- Commitment

Figure 2 *The performance 'sandwich'*

The rest of this book divides performance management into four stages:

1. Chapters 2 and 3 examine the needs for enhanced business performance and capability and how organisations are delivering the solutions to these needs.
2. Chapters 4 to 10 examine the performance cycle in detail. The performance cycle is the key mechanism by which managers manage the performance of their staff.
3. Chapters 11 to 14 examine the support that the organisation needs to give its managers in the form of effective policies and processes to recruit, retain and reward high performing staff and also how to design organisations in which people spend time on achieving business objectives rather than dissipate it on pointless administration and inter-departmental conflicts.
4. Chapter 15 looks at how effective performance management processes can be introduced.

2

The Components of Business Performance

Before we examine some of the important elements in the management of performance, it is important to try to identify what performance is required by organisations in relation to their business. One of the main criticisms of performance management systems is that they have failed to measure the performance requirements of their organisation or, at least, they have described those needs in such woolly terms that they have left both parties in the appraisal process saying 'so what?' at the end of the interview.

A major clearing bank had the following as its appraisal criteria:

Assessment of performance
Use of skills and knowledge
Initiative and organising ability
Team working and adaptability
Customer service

This list was supported by a series of boxes for each factor and the whole appraisal rested on the marking of a series of boxes from A to E – A being reserved for exceptional performance, C represented a good year's work and E for performance designated as 'less than acceptable'. One could conduct many such interviews on these criteria without really getting to the root of business performance – either performance required or performance delivered. At a more senior level, these criteria were translated into:

Achievement and output
Professional competence
Staff management
Business management

This was a nod in the right direction but even so, there seems little opportunity to acknowledge the specific company's needs for performance and how those needs might be fulfilled.

The point which seems to be missed by many organisations about managing performance is the need to focus attention on certain key issues. The process of performance management is the ideal vehicle through which to enhance and develop performance in a strategic direction and not towards some vague motherhood concepts such as team-building and organising ability.

KEY ISSUES OF PERFORMANCE MANAGEMENT

Performance management should be aiming to clarify the organisation's needs for business performance and setting up a process which ensures that it is delivered. This can only be done with a high level of strategic alignment of all the processes involved in the management and development of people throughout the whole organisation. Each policy, procedure, system and process which relates to the development of people must be mutually reinforcing if the organisation is to ensure that a clear message goes out about the direction in which it is going and the individual performance which is required to enable it to get there. Any deviation from the organisation's mission dissipates that message so that top management have to carry out a shepherding process – trying to find strays and point them in the right direction – rather than working as charioteers, directing a harnessed team towards their goal as effectively as possible.

In a time of change, business strategies need two key perspectives: 1) achieving today's performance and 2) developing the organisation to take on the challenge of tomorrow so that current performance can be exceeded in the future. This is one of the important differences between performance management and several 'management by objectives' (MBO) programmes that exist. MBO normally concentrates on the quantitative and the short term at the expense of the qualitative and the long term; performance management concentrates on both, which is exactly what business organisations need. The key concepts of performance and capability need to be kept under close review in all types of organisation – in the short term to ensure survival, and in the long term to ensure the growth necessary to facilitate long-term survival.

Before moving on to explore these key concepts it is necessary to explore, in simple terms, how the main business strategies require both performance management and capability development if they are to be fully effective. I have taken as my model the three key generic strategies referred to by Michael Porter in his book *Competitive Advantage* – Cost Leadership, Differentiation and Focus.

Cost leadership

Cost leadership, where an organisation seeks to be the low-cost producer in its industry, is a strategy which requires close control of cost performance on a regular basis and constant incremental reduction in costs without damaging other aspects of the business. If the organisation is not to damage the other elements of its business then it must also institute long-term improvements in capability, such as productivity improvements, implementation of new systems and training and development of staff, so that cost reductions can be achieved by business improvements rather than by unthinking application of the accountant's pen.

Differentiation

Differentiation is a strategy whereby an organisation seeks to be unique in its market place by being significantly better at all aspects of their business which are highly prized by the buyer. Differentiators are not cost-immune but must create a differential of such significance that it makes their cost position less important to the buyer. Differentiation can take many forms:

- Customer service
- Design
- Distribution
- Product quality
- Product reliability
- Product durability
- Technology
- Value for money
- Product exclusivity
- Product range
- Retail support
- Product/company image
- Responsiveness
- Product innovation
- Innovative packaging

The differentiators are known as *critical success factors* – the things that the organisation needs to do well in order to compete effectively in their market.

A differentiation strategy only remains effective while the differential is maintained and while it is still relevant to the buyer. This implies that short-term performance improvement must be maintained whilst, in the longer term, setting up processes to ensure that the differential remains relevant and continues to meet customer needs whilst still retaining control of costs.

Focus

Another key strategy is the *niche* or *focus* strategy. This involves selecting a segment within an industry and concentrating effort on achieving competitive advantage in that particular sector, even though the organisation may not be a market leader in their particular field. Niche products normally have high margins to compensate for lack of scale in production or distribution. They must, however, be a genuine niche product with a clear focus and not just a small player in the industry as a whole. The focus strategy must be either a *cost leader* (because they don't have the high overheads of a large organisation) or a *differential* (otherwise they won't be able to charge high prices for their perceived product benefits). The focus strategy needs good performance today, to control costs or maintain benefits, and it also needs to build in effective long-term development to ensure that the niche and the company hold on it remains strong.

Each of these business strategies require certain types of performance which the organisation's performance management process needs to deliver. This book is not about corporate strategy – Michael Porter has developed that niche very effectively without any help from me. A brief review of corporate strategy does, however, lead us to a number of conclusions about the need for effective performance within organisations:

- Organisations need to maintain a balance between performance and capability. To focus on performance to the exclusion of capability (ie short term instead of long term), is to run the risk of being taken by surprise by changes in the future and being condemned to a reactive, rather than a proactive, role. In the same way, concentrating on long-term development at the expense of the short term is to run the risk of tripping up over insignificant performance issues and the possibility of not having a future to work in.
- Each organisation must have a clear idea of the critical success factors in their industry and must set up management processes which concentrate on and achieve those factors. Generic performance measures are of little use in an organisation; there needs to be a clear understanding of the specific business strategy, critical success factors and key business processes so that organisation structures and output measures will ensure survival and create growth for the future.

KEY OBJECTIVES OF PERFORMANCE MANAGEMENT

1. **Continuous improvement of business performance**
Good current business performance is important because it enables the organisation to survive – the most basic requirement of an effective organisation. Most organisations in the United Kingdom are in a competitive environment and so survival is not merely an academic issue, especially as their environment is becoming more, rather than less, competitive. Even hospitals and schools give more than a cursory glance towards the activities of their competitors.
The most effective organisations have encapsulated their current performance needs in a *mission statement* – a statement of what the organisation is here to do. The measure of an effective organisation, as we shall see in later chapters, does not relate solely to profit. Other critical success factors need to be met in order to ensure that profit remains high enough both to guarantee survival and to create the possibility of future growth. An organisation must ensure profitability by having an income which more than exceeds its expenditure. It can only do this by continuous improvement in the areas which it regards as critical to success such as customer service or product quality, and by setting targets in those areas, reviewing the results and re-targeting when the desired results have been achieved.
2. **Continuous development of organisational capability**
The development of organisational capability is the other half of the task of the manager. It should be encapsulated in the organisation's *statement of vision* – a statement of what the organisation is likely to become. Vision is, of necessity, much broader than the concept of mission. The view of long-term capability should not stop with painting the vision, no matter how exciting or compelling that vision is. Effective management of performance involves putting into place programmes and activities which will help to convert that vision into something tangible – something that can be done by people within the organisation to prepare for the future. Setting targets for capability adds the further dimension of planning for an unpredictable future and so one of the important skill requirements within an organisation is the honing and development of the skills of strategy development.
3. **Other factors of organisational capability, as follows:**
   a) The development of systems in areas such as manufacturing, distribution and quality control which create new operating efficiencies or enhance the delivery of service.
   b) Creation of organisation structures which enable the organisation to respond more quickly to external challenges. Good, well-

designed organisation structures expedite the decision-making process and concentrate the resource and energy of the organisation on building a better business rather than dissipate it on internal debates and post-mortems.

c) Developing the competence of the people within the organisation so that their capacity to perform grows at at least the same rate as the amount of challenge imposed by the business or the market.
d) Developing new products and services and improving existing ones so that they continue to differentiate the organisation from its competitors.
e) Developing functional strategies in areas such as finance, research and human resources which support the corporate vision and create centres of excellence in key functions.
f) Setting up and maintaining systems to enhance the management of performance in the future.

The management of organisational performance cannot be fully effective until both short-term and long-term issues of both performance and capability are addressed. Short-term MBO's focusing on achievement of one or two outcome targets – sales, profit etc are dangerously flawed by encouraging a form of management myopia which fails to register much beyond the end of the next budget printout. In the days when business was 'more of the same' this type of policy may have been acceptable, although even then it was risky: now it is suicidal.

Modern businesses, whatever strategy they pursue, need a positive process which helps to manage performance across all of its dimensions. The process needs the following:

- A clear statement of the organisation's mission – ie what the organisation needs to do to compete and survive in its current business environment.
- A mechanism to enable the performance of individuals within the organisation to be aligned with that mission statement and a way of adjusting performance requirements to meet new challenges which may arise.
- A set of human resource management policies which support the organisation's strategic aims and which give the individual incentive to work towards their own personal objectives. This involves creating an environment where high performance is actively encouraged and human resource policies are in tune with corporate goals.
- A clear statement of the organisation's future goals – their vision and the direction in which they intend to move.

- A process which enables the critical capability factors within the organisation to be developed as part of the performance management process. This is particularly relevant with regard to the development of people – their competence, skills and knowledge need to be a critical part of the development of capability.

Later we will look at how these features can be achieved without creating a bureaucratic nightmare.

3

A Review of Current Performance Management Practice

Currently, performance management practice is a difficult phenomenon to pin down. It has a transient quality and most discussions on the topic start with 'well, it all depends what you mean by performance management'.

The concepts surrounding performance and the needs of organisations to achieve effective business performance whilst developing a broader capability have already been dealt with. Before examining a model for the management of performance, we need to review how organisations are responding to the needs of their business by delivering effective performance and capability.

EFFECTIVENESS OF PERFORMANCE MANAGEMENT POLICIES

High level intellectual assessment of the effectiveness of performance management policies is difficult to make. Indeed, Stephen Bevan and Marc Thompson, in their article 'Performance Management at the Crossroads' (*Personnel Management*, November 1991), concluded that, after reviewing a large sample of both private and public sector organisations, 'poor financial performers were as likely to have performance management (processes) as good performers' and that 'survey evidence points to a patchy and incomplete uptake of performance management techniques in the UK'. The IPM/IMS work pointed, however, to a number of factors which may explain this rather down-beat approach to performance management. Twenty per cent of respondents claimed to be operating a formal performance management system; a further 64 per cent did operate some policies to manage performance and the remainder had no policies in this area at all. The survey authors noted that there was no consistent definition of performance management amongst the respondents.

My own experience in this area is that many organisations carry out one aspect of a performance management process (normally performance appraisal) and then claim to operate a full performance management system. Other organisations who do manage performance and capability effectively express surprise when told that they are operating a performance management system. Part of my motivation for writing this book was the clarification of the concept of performance management for practising personnel managers and their line management colleagues.

The work on the IPM/IMS survey highlighted that the main thrust in the area of performance management for most organisations has been in performance related pay, an increasingly important trend in the 1980s and 1990s. This approach has to be contrasted with the initiatives taken by the government in the last few years in relation to a competence based approach to performance and development. These two approaches – one reward/remuneration driven; the other development and coaching driven – both emerge from the two strands of personnel management and are based on two sets of assumptions: *remuneration driven* performance management systems (see Table 1) and *development based* performance management systems.

Table 1 *Remuneration driven performance management*

Advantages

- They involve measurement and thus are likely to be less ambiguous than other processes.
- They provide clear incentives to employees to achieve results and thus add to the general stock of employee motivation. The IPM/IMS survey showed that employee motivation came second to improving organisational effectiveness as a reason for introducing a performance management system.
- The potential for directing individuals towards business objectives is high – as a tool of change management, performance related pay is potentially very effective in lubricating the levers of management within an organisation.
- Performance related pay adds some stiffening to the whole performance management process. ICL found that introducing performance related pay ensured that appraisals were carried out promptly! If nothing else, performance related pay concentrates the mind – rather like playing poker for money and not matchsticks.

Disadvantages

- Short-term-ism. The easiest results to focus on are short-term outcomes like sales, profit and cost. Long-term capability issues such as people and system development are more difficult to measure within a time scale which is relevant for performance related pay. The impact of performance related pay is to underline short-term business issues at the expense of the long term.
- Individual based performance related pay programmes often focus an individual's attention on their own set of accountabilities to the exclusion of the work of others, thus working against effective team-building. This can, of course, be mitigated by introducing PRP schemes based on team or unit performance. A key point is that performance related pay schemes can work *too* well in directing performance and that if the scheme isn't well designed it may have unforeseen consequences as people work hard to maximise their income.
- Performance related pay can be expensive if it is not designed correctly. Organisations need to ensure that they are not just paying more for an unspecified benefit – otherwise the return on the performance pay programme may not equal the costs of implementing the programme.

Performance related pay has worked effectively but there are several criteria that need to be met before a scheme can be seriously developed. There must be a clear sense of organisational mission with a set of critical success factors underpinning it. An organisation needs to know what performance it requires before it can design the necessary incentives to achieve it. Jobs must have the flexibility for people to affect their personal performance, and headroom in which to expand that contribution to the corporate mission. There must be effective measures of performance – quantitative and qualitative – as well as clear statements about the behaviour required to influence those measures.

Development Based Performance Management

Development based performance management has been less utilised than performance related pay. Over the last decade, this approach has been encouraged through various government sponsored initiatives in vocational training and education. The work of bodies such as the Management Charter Initiative has used the competence approach as a basis for training, assessment and appraisal.

It is important here to define *competence* and *competency*. The dictionary makes no distinction between the nuances of the two words, although management development specialists have. Richard Boyatzis' book *The Competent Manager* (John Wiley, 1982) began to use the two words in a distinctly different way:

> *Competence* – is used to describe areas of work in which the individual is competent, relating particularly to the tasks they carry out at work.
> *Competency* – the traits or characteristics of a person which enable them to perform their job successfully – Boyatzis refers to 'underlying characteristics of a person' and 'motive, trait, skill, aspect of one's self-image or social role or a body of knowledge which he or she uses'.

The one word (competence) relates to what people need to do to perform effectively in their current role; the other word (competency) relates to the potential to transfer those skills to other areas. Both of these factors are critical in relation to the management of performance: competence is a necessary condition of performance, people can only perform well if they have the necessary skills and knowledge to do the job; competency is a key capability factor, people can only develop new skills if they possess the personal characteristics which can be transferred into higher quality work.

The disadvantage of a development based approach is that it may lack the methodology to ensure that competence is directed towards today's need for business performance and that competency is developing the skills that the organisation needs for the future.

Other Approaches

Some organisations adopt other performance management approaches –

Succession/manpower planning some organisations have used the succession planning process to drive effective performance management. Succession planning addresses organisational capability at a macro-level and then focuses more closely on what needs to be done to put the succession plan into practice. In order to be fully effective, succession planning needs to draw together competence analysis, training needs analysis and development review discussions – an issue we will review later in the book.

Total quality management TQM has been the route to performance management for some organisations. The key concepts of TQM – continuous improvement, supplier/customer internal contracts and effective management control by use of management information systems are equally valid within performance management and need to be built into performance management systems to make them work effectively. Organisations with an effective TQM perspective normally have had the necessary prerequisites in place to facilitate the implementation of performance management programmes.

Bevan and Thomson say in their article (see page 31): 'Performance management is at a crossroads in UK organisations.' Their view is that the crossroads is between 'reward-driven integration' and 'development-driven integration'; currently their findings point to a move towards reward-driven integration. A concern that they have is that this will result in short-termism, the same complaint that afflicted management by objectives.

My view is that there is a need to synthesise the full range of current approaches. Each one brings something to the party – remuneration systems if directed towards the achievement of the corporate mission brings effective measurement of business performance and employee motivation; development approaches encourage the long-term development of the individual and their self-fulfilment; succession plans encourage future development planning and total quality management helps to bind individual plans together in a coherent whole and to generate an ethos of continuous improvement.

We can now move on to examine how these features can be integrated to create a 'total performance management' process for the future.

4

The Performance Cycle

Traditionally, performance has been managed sporadically. It seems that most managers operate on two cycles – the longer term annual appraisal and the day-to-day, 'up to your arse in alligators' crisis management. Somewhere between these two extremes, there must be a better way.

TRADITIONAL APPROACHES TO PERFORMANCE MANAGEMENT

The two traditional approaches to performance management are the annual appraisal and day-to-day assessment.

Performance appraisal is undoubtedly a 'good thing'. It is, however, a system which has become loaded with every management function imaginable, so that it has become an interview with so many objectives that it is not surprising that it is approached with dread by both parties. The annual appraisal is still, in many organisations, the prime mechanism for the following:

- Reviewing performance over the last year;
- Setting targets for the next year;
- Identifying training needs;
- Discussing career development opportunities;
- Reviewing the job and seeing if there is a better way to carry it out;
- Agreeing merit pay increases.

If the interview lasts two to three hours, that equates to around half an hour per year of reflective discussion for each of those topics. As a practising personnel manager, I spent many hours trying to unravel appraisal systems and create some sense out of their bureaucracy. Many organisations have sensed that opportunities are lost during the appraisal interview but instead of changing the process, they have concentrated on training people to operate the system better. This is rather like the owner of a battered old car taking advanced driving lessons in order to win the Le Mans 24 Hour race. We need to change the system if we are to improve the management of performance.

First, we need to change the view that the management of performance is an annual event. The concept of an annual appraisal must have been developed in more leisurely days when business changed slowly and a year was a reasonable gestation time for new projects. I began to question the validity of the annual appraisal at a reasonably early stage in my career when I was the victim of a traditional appraisal interview. We spent the first twenty minutes reviewing the key targets that I had been set at my last interview. The first target I had completed within two weeks of the initial interview; the second target had become irrelevant at an early stage in the year and scrapped in favour of some other project; the third – well, neither of us could remember what had happened to it: it had become an OBE (Overtaken By Events). The interview was not particularly fruitful – something like 95% of my previous year's work was discounted, a fact which I had to drag into the discussion. We spent the first half hour trying to examine progress on projects which had become irrelevant. We spent a desultory half hour discussing my future which was also irrelevant as I was about to attend the final interview for a job in another organisation!

How can the annual performance appraisal be a positive contribution to the company's strategic direction if the first part is spent trawling back through history?

Day-to-day **crisis management** is where targets are set daily and feedback given in the manner of a Roman Emperor appraising gladiators – thumbs up or thumbs down. This type of performance management is equally unsatisfactory – more, in Philip Crosby's famous phrase from *Quality is Free* (New American Library, 1974), 'like ice-hockey than ballet'. Masses of activity, the constant flow of adrenalin – anthill management, moving and buzzing in circles – with unsatisfying feedback given off the cuff.

The answer to these two extremes is a constant and disciplined management of performance which I have called the *performance cycle* (see Figure 3).

THE PERFORMANCE CYCLE APPROACH

There are several important principles which I believe differentiate the performance cycle approach from some of the other performance

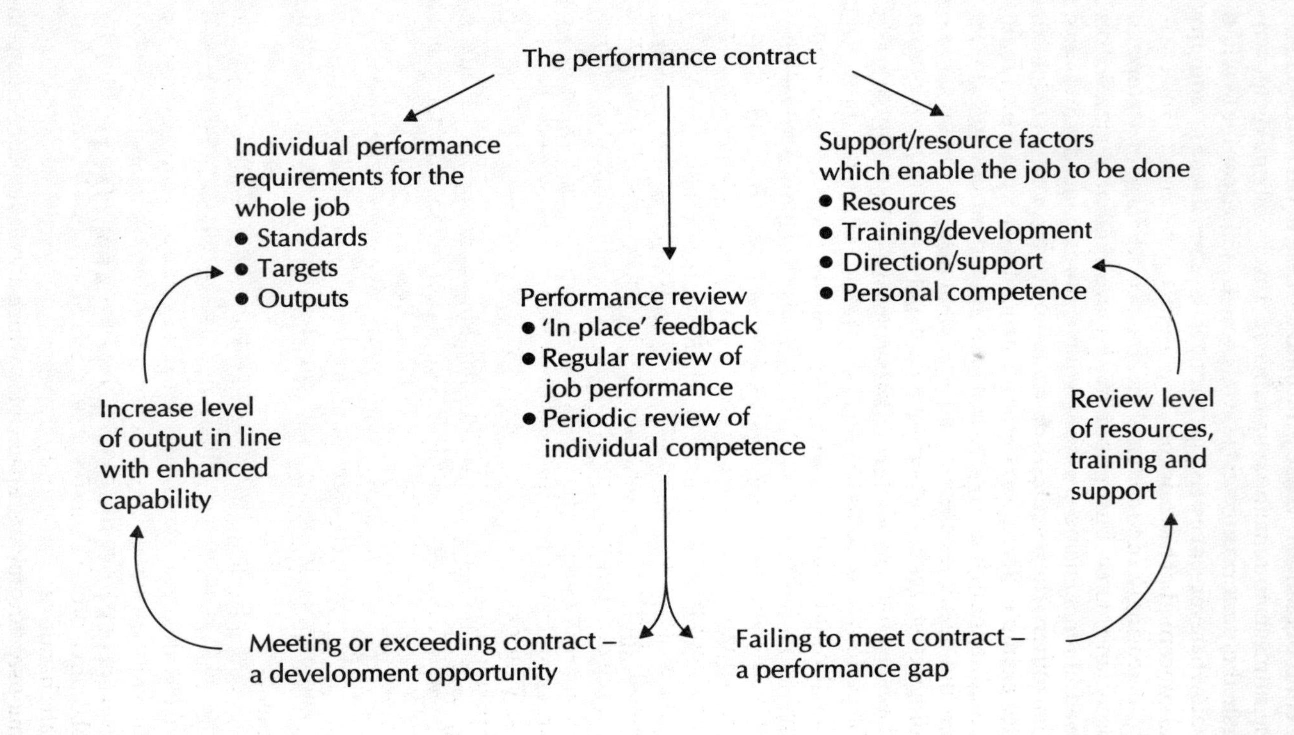

Figure 3 *Performance management cycle*

management programmes. These principles are essential if the organisation of the future is to remain competitive in today's business environment. First, the performance cycle is a process which can be worked through at whatever speed is appropriate to the business and the individual concerned. The concept of an annual performance review is becoming increasingly out-moded. Performance needs to be managed more closely and some businesses need more regular reviews than others. In addition, some people need to have more regular performance reviews than others; the less experienced or those who need considerable support for example. The cycle of performance has no particular timescale attached, although as we shall see it is important to agree review dates to ensure deadlines are met. The cycle emphasises the need to go through different stages in the performance management approach on an iterative basis, so that any change in performance or environment leads back to the performance contract – the key stage in the cycle.

Secondly, the performance cycle ensures that everyone's performance is managed in all areas of their work. In my experience, traditional performance management approaches have focused on two sets of performers – high fliers, whose career development needs must be fulfilled; and poor performers, where the performance gap needs to be reduced. The majority of people, the 'about standard' performers, gain very little at all apart from insincere thanks and the possibility of a training course as a reward for loyal service. High fliers, who meet their targets with ease, are immediately re-targeted with a more challenging set of performance requirements; poor performers become the subject of a joint problem-solving exercise and an overall review of the reasons for the apparent performance gap; the mainstream performers who are meeting their performance contract are treated to a little of both – support for those areas of their work that they find more difficult, raised targets for those areas that they accomplish with ease. In this way, no-one is left coasting, there is always a goal to aim for. This not only creates a sense of continuous development in the individual, it also creates a pattern of continuous improvement in the business by a series of incremental improvements.

The process is a cycle and not a cascade. It is a joint process between two people, one of whom is the boss, the other the subordinate. As we shall see later, the cycle starts with the development of a performance contract in which an agreed level of output is required but balanced by an agreed level of support by the boss for the person producing the output. This collaborative process should go on throughout the relationship with a systematic handover of authority from boss to subordinate on the basis of continuously improving levels of performance and continuously developing levels of competence.

Stage 1 – The performance contract

I recently made a significant career change. After several years as a personnel manager with various organisations, I resigned from my position with a division of a clearing bank to become an independent management development consultant. I agreed, however, with my employer to remain with them for a short period in order to carry out certain projects. We agreed on the work I was to do, a reasonably precise statement of the performance required from me, some interim deadlines and a fee for the work. I drafted a note summarising our agreement. I duly completed these projects to the required specification, was paid promptly and moved on to other projects.

This was very different from the relationship that I had enjoyed with all my previous employers. My time as a personnel manager (employed) was characterised by unclear objectives, deadlines which were vague until they became critical ('I need that report on my desk *tomorrow*') and sporadic supervision.

My subsequent experience as a consultant has confirmed my first assignment to be the norm: short contracts, clear objectives and well-defined outcomes. This is generally the nature of any consultancy contract, whereby employees, particularly those in 'staff' functions, work on long-term contracts, essentially to do whatever they are asked to do with an (often) ill-defined set of outcomes.

Many writers have also identified that a psychological contract exists between the organisation and the people within it. This contract, as any other business contract, is based on the expectations and obligations of both parties so that they will gain some mutual benefit from working together. The individual has a series of outcomes that they expect from their work in the organisation, the achievement of which will satisfy some of their needs and in return they will generate some form of agreed output in support of the organisations objectives. Those contracts, however, may operate in different ways – based on a mixture of coercion, calculation or co-operation.

Essentially, the *coercive* contract occurs when the individual is expected to conform and comply with the organisation's culture in return for the avoidance of punishment. *Calculative* contracts are those in which parties recognise, on the basis of dispassionate calculation, that it is in their mutual interest to work together. In the third type of contract, based on *co-operation*, the individual identifies with the goals of the organisation and expends their energies quite voluntarily in pursuit of those goals, partly for the enjoyment of being involved with the organisation.

Different organisations are based on different forms of the psychological contract. Coercive organisations are normally military or penal in nature but may include some highly regulated business organisations. At the other end of the scale, purely co-operative organisations tend to be charities and voluntary bodies. Most organisations, however, need a blend of the three types of contract in order to not only retain the energy of the individuals, but to do so with their full commitment.

Business organisations, if they are to be fully effective, need a bias towards contracts based on co-operation. However, managers may have to impose sanctions at an early stage of creating an organisational strategy to coerce those people within the organisation who may not be prepared to follow that strategy voluntarily. For example, an organisation putting renewed emphasis on customer service may need to discipline people within the organisation who provide flawed examples of customer care.

Most organisations are likely to create a contract which is a mixture of calculative and co-operative. This is important for performance management because the logical, calculating element of the brain needs to be harnessed with its creative and emotional side in order to create total commitment. People need both to feel committed to the goals of their organisation because they have made a contribution to setting those goals, as well as feeling that they actually gain something tangible by working effectively towards them.

The contract, therefore, needs to have this blend of co-operation and calculation. Managing by contract should be extended throughout, between and within the people of an organisation; between departments within the organisation; and, in particular, between the managers and their staff. These contracts exist whether we acknowledge them or not. In Contract Law, contracts are deemed to exist even though they may only be implied, provided that people are operating as if the contracts exist. Implied contracts should become clearly stated contracts as often as possible. It is not enough to believe that these contracts exist; it is essential to formalise and clarify them and to use them as the basis for an effective working relationship.

An external contract between a customer and a supplier would clarify the range and quantity of services to be delivered, the product quality and delivery schedule. It would also build in some mechanism for handling disputes and may anticipate some potential problems and how they might be resolved. In the same way, the performance contract between a manager and a member of his team and between functions within an organisation, should set out performance requirements along with the obligations and expectations of both parties. It should set out when the contract should be reviewed and how possible conflicts of interest may be reconciled. This can be written down and used as a permanent record of the 'terms of business' between the two parties. It is neither bureaucratic nor impersonal. It would certainly not need to be drafted by a lawyer but it should be clear enough that both parties understand what is expected of them and what they can expect from the relationship.

Managing by contract is an important factor in performance management.

- It focuses on the whole job or relationship.
- It clarifies issues rather than leaving them fuzzy.
- It formulates relationships at the outset rather than by 'ex post facto' rationalisation ('No, I understood that you would be providing that ...').
- It is two-sided and invests both parties to the agreement with rights and responsibilities.

Managing by contract should apply throughout the organisation with everyone agreeing a performance contract with their boss, setting out principal performance requirements, clarifying the resources available to them, the training and development they need to achieve their performance target and the amount of direction and support they will need from their boss.

Stage 2 – Clarifying performance requirements

The contract is between two parties and consists of two elements – the clarification of performance requirements and the agreement of the corresponding support in terms of resources, training and direction from the manager. The individual needs to know what output is required of them in order to prevent some of the dreadful misunderstandings which are created when people quite simply do not know what is expected of them.

There are a few concepts that we need to understand if we are to set appropriate objectives which will take the organisation forward. Setting these objectives carefully will form the basis for a range of other performance management functions – the management of reward in particular, and so should be carried out with great care. The key points are as follows.

The performance requirements in a performance contract are for the whole job and not just selected parts of it The process of clarifying requirements starts by sketching out the boundaries of the job – these are always likely to be sketchy because job boundaries can get fuzzy around the edges in a growing, dynamic business. The process goes on to define more closely the critical success factors of the job, which relate to the whole job – they will not clarify the details of the job activities but should state quite clearly the areas of activity in which high performance is critical. Performance requirements should be set for these critical success factors in measurable terms and these become the performance requirements for the performance contract.

Performance targets which focus only on one or two elements of the job run the risk of distorting job performance in order to maximise reward. For example, many food retailers have bonus schemes for store managers which focus on outcomes such as sales and profit, ignoring other critical success factors such as customer service, hygiene, staff development and so on. It can be argued that profitability is a consequence of good customer care, stock availability, staff motivation and so on and thus a legitimate measure of effectiveness. Like most managers, I know of several ways in which the bottom line can be distorted for a period at the expense of the long-term effectiveness of the business. If we want staff development, good use of assets, hygiene, quality and all those other important things, we should ask for them as part of the performance contract and not hope that they will be achieved if the bottom line profit is adequate.

Performance requirements are made up of a blend of standards and targets
Standards are universal, targets are individual and specific and ideally our performance requirements should consist of both elements. The performance contract is individual, although it should embody the standards of performance which apply to the work group as a whole, but with additional elements for each individual to stretch them further in some aspects of their work. People work at different levels of ability and it is important that their performance requirements reflect those disparities and provide sufficient challenge to motivate them as individuals without driving people beyond their level of competence.

Stage 3 – Agreeing support requirements

The element present in the concept of the performance contract, which always seems to be missing elsewhere in management, is the mutuality of the contract. In the management by command style, the element of support is forgotten. There should be two sides to a performance contract in order to ensure balance and to generate commitment. If you see your boss prepared to offer help and support in achieving your aims, the impact of your level of commitment cannot help but increase.

Support comes in many forms:

- Resources – there is a need to review the level of resources required to achieve the performance requirements – an important factor in performance management. Performance management is not just about achieving more with less, although this can happen incrementally if continuous improvement processes are built in to the performance contract. It is the avoidance of giving unreasonable output targets to be achieved with minimal resources. Turning Sisyphus into Hercules and asking for the Augean stables to be cleaned out with a hand brush is not the way to achieve effective performance.

- Training – we have already established that people cannot perform beyond their level of competence; it is important, therefore, that managers should contract with their team to provide an appropriate amount of training and coaching to enable them to fulfil their part of the contract. This need not be formal 'classroom' training but may cover a range of possible training methods, including management coaching. If we agree that the training and development of people rests with the manager, then it is not unreasonable for the manager to clarify the nature of the training and build it into the performance contract.

  A further reason for including training needs in the performance contract is that it helps ensure that the individual's training needs relate to the performance that is required of them, either now or in the future. This helps to keep training needs fully relevant and builds in a more effective form of training evaluation, ie how does it help them do the job better?
- Management style – this is what Hersey and Blanchard in *Management of Organisational Behaviour* call 'contracting for leadership style'. Essentially the manager should agree with the individual at the contracting stage, the level of support and direction that they need to carry out their performance requirements, given their current level of competence and their commitment to the work they are expected to do. People need to know how they will be managed and discussing this as a part of the performance contract helps to ensure that this is done consistently. The style contract should also be reviewed regularly with the aim of giving people more freedom by moving from a directive 'supervisory' style to a more relaxed coaching approach, all the while delegating more work in order to free up the manager's time.

Stage 4 – Reviewing performance

When the contract has been agreed it needs to be regularly reviewed. This review should normally be carried out at three levels. Firstly, 'in place' feedback delivered by the manager when things go well or badly. This is delivered very simply in the form of praise or constructive criticism.

Secondly, there needs to be a regular review of job performance; a review of the performance contract. At the performance review meeting the manager should give feedback to the individual or discuss the performance requirements against agreed targets, as well as discuss the amount of training and development or direction and support that the individual has received and may need in the future. The review is a good opportunity to set higher targets when appropriate. Finally, there should be a periodic review of individual competence; performance appraisal. This is not the same as a review of performance against targets. The latter relates to the job and the contract; the annual or periodic appraisal of individual competence is an examination of the individual and their development to meet present and future performance requirements.

Stages 5 & 6 – Meeting or exceeding contract

People either exceed, meet or fail to meet their contract. For purposes of performance management, I believe that meeting the contract is the same as exceeding it insofar as it implies achievement of the current performance requirements. For continuous improvement, achievement of a set of objectives should trigger the agreement of a new set of objectives, otherwise people tend to stagnate because achievement of their objectives creates no response; in fact, they may get less attention than the poor performers who do at least receive some feedback on their performance.

Managers should see the achievement of a set of performance requirements as a staging camp on the way to excellence. Meeting their contract is an important achievement but it should suggest to the line manager that there is scope for attaining new goals for staff and, by definition, themselves. It is a development opportunity for the business, for the individual and the manager. Good performers create business growth and this needs to be augmented by a process of delegation from which everyone can benefit – the business by benefiting from greater output, the individual by working on more challenging projects and the manager, both by increasing his team's output overall and by having someone to whom more of his own work can be delegated.

The key to working effectively in this loop is to increase performance requirements by small steps across the range of performance areas rather than distort the balance of the job by asking for a massive improvement in one area. The aim of this process is to create a series of small successes which gradually build up into a significant success. Contracts can always be reviewed and increased again if they prove to be too easy, but they cannot so easily be reduced if both the individual and manager feel that this represents backing down. Increasing the target poses a challenge; decreasing it implies failure.

Stages 7 & 8 – Failing to meet contract

These stages outline one of the typical performance management problems. The solution is to reapply the familiar problem-solving loop (explore the gap, agree an action plan, etc) in a fresh way. The problem-solving must be a joint effort between manager and team member because both parties have a problem – the manager, because poor performance from a team member may prevent his meeting his contract (an effective organisation cascades performance contracts) and the subordinate, who almost certainly feels uneasy and unfulfilled. Both parties need to work to review the gap between current and required performance; first examining the support side of the contract, then adjusting the performance requirements. There needs to be a review of resources – are they enough? Is the manager providing enough direction or support?

Another possible problem is the amount of feedback or review time. The solution may be simply to increase the regularity and specificity of the feedback in order to give clearer direction and develop greater confidence.

Problem-solving needs adequate analysis, the generation and testing of hypotheses and the agreement on a solution, which itself must be embedded in a revised performance contract. As a last resort, the performance requirements may be changed. Last resort because this in itself can create problems; accusations of bias or unfairness relative to other members of the team, loss of confidence by the individual and a failure to meet contract on the part of the boss.

We will now move on to review each of the stages of the performance management cycle in detail, with suggestions on agendas for change.

5

Agreeing the Performance Requirements

The performance contract is the basis of effective performance management and therefore must be clear and measurable. A well produced performance contract acts as a springboard for a range of other issues – performance appraisal, reward management and business planning. The idea of the contract focusing on the whole job is particularly important in relation to reward management. Many bonuses or performance related pay programmes distort performance by focusing on one set of outputs or outcomes. This often creates an unbalanced set of performance measures because individuals may ignore, or at least underperform in, some areas of their job in order to maximise their bonus. Quantitative production-related bonuses can have a disastrous effect not only on product quality but also on the balance sheet as a whole by producing surplus goods.

The only way to ensure a balanced performance, fully consonant with the organisation's aims is to set and manage performance requirements for the whole job. Staff development is often ignored in large organisations because it rarely figures in a performance related pay scheme or any measurable set of targets. It would, however, be an important feature in a performance contract and thus take its place alongside financial management, service management and product quality as something that managers need to work on if they are to be paid their bonus.

Staff development is also not an issue in some performance programmes because it is usually inadequately measured and so it is critical that the performance requirements are clear and unambiguous. The individual should leave the performance contract meeting armed with a clear idea of the performance that is required of them for the future across the full range of their work. This will be balanced by an agreement of the training and support that they can expect to receive to help them achieve

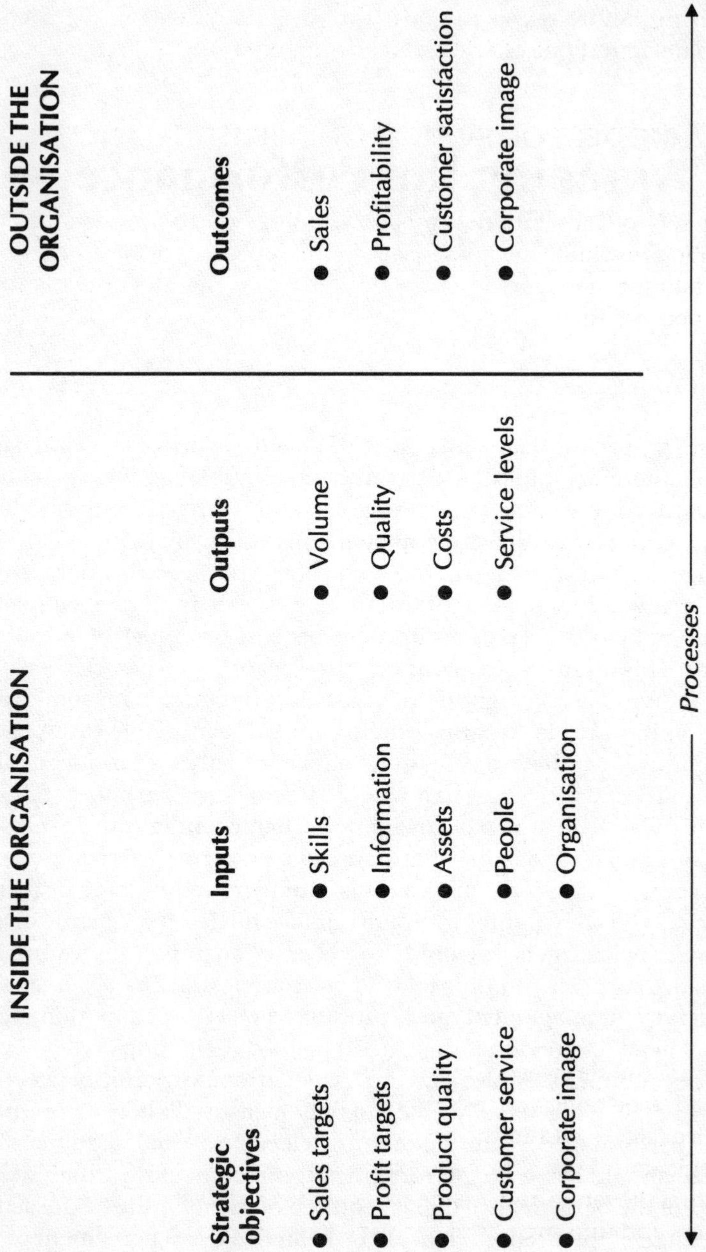

INSIDE THE ORGANISATION			OUTSIDE THE ORGANISATION
Strategic objectives	**Inputs**	**Outputs**	**Outcomes**
• Sales targets	• Skills	• Volume	• Sales
• Profit targets	• Information	• Quality	• Profitability
• Product quality	• Assets	• Costs	• Customer satisfaction
• Customer service	• People	• Service levels	• Corporate image
• Corporate image	• Organisation		

← *Processes* →

Figure 4 *A model for evaluating performance*

those requirements. The means they use to carry out those methods should be largely a matter for their own discretion within the boundaries set for them. Before reviewing how this is done, however, we need to clarify some definitions of effective performance.

A MODEL FOR EVALUATING PERFORMANCE

Figure 4 sets out a simplified model to enable us to understand how organisations evaluate the immensely complex process of performance. It is important for managers to understand the key factors in the management of performance.

Strategic objectives

The strategic objectives or 'mission', as they are collectively known, are a statement of an organisation's basic purpose. The mission statement summarises the direction in which an organisation wishes to go and sets out the priorities when strategic decisions are being made.

Inputs

Inputs are what an organisation needs in order to produce the products or services which are highlighted in the strategic objectives. Specifically, they are assets, systems, people, organisation structures and information. These areas cannot achieve strategic objectives in themselves but, like petrol and oil in a car, they have an important role to play in relation to the achievement of results – particularly in the long term. Inputs are the capability factors in the organisation; the infrastructure in a country; and competence in relation to the individual. They are also likely to be the main cost elements within an organisation.

Outputs

Outputs are the services and products which the organisation produces. They need to be reviewed in terms of volume, quality and cost. They are the service factors within the organisation and need to be closely related to strategic objectives. They are normally the items in the organisation which attract revenue and are the basis of the organisations 'offer' to their consumers and thus are particularly measurable for the organisation and the managers within it.

Processes

Processes are the systems and procedures which convert inputs into outputs. For example, training is one of the processes which converts people into managers. An awareness of the importance of process within an organisation is critical and all processes need to be subjected to critical review in order to ensure that they remain in line with the strategic objectives and mission of the organisation.

Outcomes

Outcomes are distinct from outputs in a particularly important way. *Outputs* are purposive and therefore controllable within the organisation. *Outcomes* are consequential, the results of performance, and are outside the direct control of the organisation. For example, in health care, performing a successful heart by-pass operation is an output, the quality of life and subsequent increased life expectancy would be an outcome. In commercial terms, sales volume, profitability, customer satisfaction and corporate image are all examples of outcomes. Whilst affected by corporate output, nevertheless they are ultimately beyond the complete control of the organisation, as they depend on the reaction of consumers to the organisation's output.

Organisational performance is affected by efficiency, quality, responsiveness, cost effectiveness and overall effectiveness.

Efficiency a comparison of output against input. The aim of efficiency is to get more output for the same input. It is simple and relatively easy to measure; its main weakness as a measure of performance is its lack of relevance to either strategic objectives or outcomes. A product or service that no-one wants, however efficiently produced, is ineffective.

Quality Quality is a measure of both output and process. It relates to the concept of 'fitness for purpose' or 'conformance to requirements'. It relates the quality of the product or service to the needs of the customer, and should therefore be an effective measure of organisational responsiveness to customer needs.

Responsiveness Do strategic objectives change in response to outcomes which fail to meet expectations? In other words, is there an effective feedback mechanism from the external environment which enables the organisation to react quickly?

Cost effectiveness This is a comparison between outcomes and their relation to inputs. It is a stronger test than efficiency because it relates to the *impact* of the inputs on achieving overall objectives. Typically this would include measures of, for example, Return on Capital Employed where the outcome (profit) is related to inputs (capital) – an important measure of cost effectiveness. This category is the one most used to review the financial effectiveness of an organisation.

Effectiveness An all-embracing measure taking in all the others. It has particular relevance in non-profit organisations where measures of 'profitability' are notional or non-existent. Effectiveness is a comparison of outcomes against strategic objectives, in other words, does the organisation achieve what it set out to achieve? All the other measures relate to this but are not all-embracing. Efficiency is not important if the organisation is not achieving the expected outcomes; quality is not important if the organisation cannot achieve quality within cost constraints; cost effectiveness may lack an effective set of strategic objectives to drive long-term effectiveness. None of the other measures is able to stand alone as a comprehensive review of corporate performance.

To be effective, as we said earlier, organisations need to balance inputs, outputs and outcomes in order to ensure that they remain effective. Without strategic objectives the organisation has no target and no clear view of the performance it wants to achieve. It becomes outcome driven and without clear objectives, any outcome which exceeds that of the previous year by inflation + 5% becomes satisfactory.

Without understanding inputs an organisation may not be putting in place the infrastructure for sustained high level performance. Inputs (staff, assets, organisation structure and so on) should be seen as those aspects of corporate strategy which relate to the long-term capability of the organisation and so investments in manpower and technology must be seen as building up long-term growth.

If an organisation does not focus on outputs, it may not last until tomorrow! Clear output orientation ensures that an organisation is performance-focused and concentrating its attention on products and services rather than focusing too much on inessentials.

Finally, if clear information about outcomes is not available the organisation becomes less responsive and is unable to adjust its strategic objectives to meet changing circumstances. Outcomes for a commercial organisation may not always be measurable in terms of profit or sales and these qualitative outcomes (customer satisfaction, corporate image etc.) need to be clarified as closely as the quantative measures.

Before moving away from the performance model, it is important to clarify several other issues. The model should be viewed, as should almost all the concepts raised in this book, at both macro- and micro-level – the level of the whole organisation and of individual managers within it.

In the same way that organisations need to be aware of the interplay between objectives, inputs, outputs and outcomes, so do individual managers. In the organisational framework there are some managers whose function and performance is likely to be seen as a contribution to the 'input' side of the balance sheet – personnel managers, market researchers, IT managers and so forth. These are the cost centres, the administrators who stay at home while the sales and production people (who are all 'output' people) go out and win the business to create profit centres.

Ideally, all employees need to be aware of both output and input. As a production manager, you may have some input objectives that need to be dealt with – a staffing matter for example. This is an input objective for you, but for your personnel manager it will probably be an output objective – for example, to provide people who are skilled and ready to work to 90% capacity within 6 weeks. Every output objective relating to the maintenance, development or improvement of a product or service should be underpinned by a corresponding input or capability objective to ensure that it can remain fully effective for the future. Every job should have a mixture of input and output requirements. Without output a job has no rationale; without input it has no future. Jobs which are seen as 'input-oriented' can also use the process to create their own performance edge. For example, in Figure 5 I have applied the model to a training function.

This approach has the effect of creating greater awareness on the part of the section or function of the service it provides and the impact of managing that service.

AGREEING PERFORMANCE REQUIREMENTS

The performance evaluation model is a theoretical model, for which I apologise. It is, however, important to understand the different elements of performance and the way that effectiveness should be judged. Performance management programmes often focus on outcomes and fail to clarify some of the outputs which comprise those outcomes. It is a process of simple analysis, asking some critical questions at each stage. My aim here is to take the jargon out of the process.

Many of the managers that I have worked with both as a personnel manager and, lately, as a management consultant often express concern that the performance management process is made excessively complex by people such as myself. My reply has to be that the concepts are relatively simple but that if we are to do an effective job of clarifying performance requirements then we need to do some rigorous analysis of

INTRA-DEPARTMENTAL			OUTSIDE THE DEPARTMENT
Strategic objectives	**Inputs**	**Outputs**	**Outcomes**
1. Development of a training conference facility	1.1 Completion of audio-visual system by X date	1.1 Availability of conference facility 1.2 Costs of conference facility	1.1 Utilisation of conference facility
2. Supporting the implementation of new systems	2.1 Design and develop open learning programme on new system	2.1 Percentage of staff fully trained within X weeks of system live date	2.1 Implementation of new system on time with error rates below X%
3. Improving the management of people within the organisation	3.1 Research available programmes 3.2 Brief consultants running programme	3.1 Percentage of managers' with training needs agreed 3.2 Percentage of managers with agreed training needs met	3.1 Reduced staff turnover 3.2 Improved staff relations (measured by attitude survey) 3.3 Increased productivity
4. Improve customer care within the organisation	4.1 Set up a team to carry out customer care training 4.2 Agree a system of pre- and post-course	4.1 Percentage of sales staff trained 4.2 Percentage of staff carried out post-course de-briefing with manager	4.1 Increase in repeat business 4.2 Increased new business 4.3 Increased customer satisfaction – measured by survey

← *Processes* →

Figure 5 *The application of the objectives, inputs, outputs, outcomes model.*

the jobs we want people to do, looking at the environment that we want them to work in and giving them some measures to enable us to judge their progress and, more importantly, to enable them to monitor their own performance. This is not a process which can be glossed over in a matter of minutes – it needs time and a high level of critical thinking.

Setting the initial performance contract is the most difficult and time consuming task if only because we are starting with a blank sheet of paper. Subsequent contract discussions are likely to be shorter. However, it is useful to hold a 'zero-based' performance contracting session, probably annually, in order to assess the relevance of the job and its context more critically and accurately.

The performance contract discussion should be built upon the following questions:

- What is the purpose of the job? (i.e. the main outcomes expected)
- What are the main boundaries of the job?
- What are the strengths and weaknesses of the job-holder? How do they relate to the needs of the business environment?
- Who are the main customers – what do they require/expect of the job holder?
- What are the main output requirements and how will we measure them?
- What do we need to be good at to enable us to achieve these requirements?

This process should draw out the main performance requirements for the job to form the basis of the contract. We will examine each of these stages in turn and include an 'agenda for change' – a pro-forma agenda for a successful contracting session.

Stage one – What is the purpose of the job?

Why does the job exist? It is important to express this in terms of its expected outcomes rather than as a bland generalised statement of the job function. Understanding that the purpose of a job is 'to manage the sales department in order to maintain turnover and ensure effective liaison with other parts of the organisation' or 'to supervise the production section of the factory in order to ensure efficient ultilisation of resources whilst maintaining product quality' is more helpful than saying that the purpose of the job is 'to manage the accounts department' or 'to research into new products'.

This is more than pure pedantry. One of the most critical factors in performance management is the change of focus from activity to results. The idea of just doing a job – managing, supervising, directing and so on implies a state of stasis – of staying still – rather than developing or improving. The concept of producing something – a product or service – is an important shift of emphasis and should be identified at an early stage in the process: not 'what are you there for?' but 'what are you there to do?'. This needs to be described in terms of outcome – sales, profit, product quality, customer satisfaction, cost control, production efficiency, staff turnover and so on. This focus on outcomes results in, first, raising the level of awareness, for both the manager and managed, of why the job exists and what the main priorities of the job should be. Secondly, it gives an initial basis for measurement of performance. Performance can be measured at two levels – output and outcomes. The former relates to the measurement of day to day services; the latter relates to wider issues which need to be measured regularly in order to ensure that the level of *output* remains appropriate and that the strategic objectives of the organisation are being met.

The position at the end of stage one should be a clear definition of the purpose of the job expressed in terms of the major outcomes for which the job holder is responsible. These outcomes then have measurable targets added to complete the overall rates of success in the job. This process should be continued in stage two.

Stage two – What are the main boundaries of the job?

Setting some major outcome targets is an important factor but before doing so it is necessary to set down clearly the boundaries of the job so that both the job holder and others have a clear idea in which areas performance is expected. Job clarity is important both for effective functioning and effective management. Essentially, this involves breaking the job down into a series of areas in which we expect the job holder to operate. I have called these *critical success factors*, although the phrase, in my experience, is largely interchangeable with key result areas.

Critical success factors are meaningful clusters of activity unique to any particular job. Normally there are between six and eight – too many begin to constitute an activity list, too few suggests a lack of thorough analysis. The critical success factors are, in terms of sketching job boundaries, the core areas of the job; literally the areas of an operation which are critical to its success. They are also the main areas in which things can go badly wrong. Huge mistakes are not often found in the detailed underbrush of the job, but rather in the high profile elements of the job for which accountability is clearly defined. The aim of the critical success factor is to be broad enough to relate to a whole 'chunk' of work whilst being specific enough to act as a guide to a new job.

Table 2 *Examples of critical success factors*

Teacher	*Head Teacher*
• Planning, organising and delivering lessons within the agreed curriculum.	• The management and development of the teaching staff.
• Curriculum planning for maths and science across the school.	• Preparing and managing the school's devolved budget.
• Making assessments on the progress of children within the class.	• Maintaining good relationships with the school's governors.
• Communication of progress to parents and education authorities.	• Ensuring the effective use and maintenance of the school's assets.
• Providing extra-mural support in music and drama.	• Ensuring compliance with local authority and central government regulations.
• Maintaining effective relationships with other staff.	• Setting up a system of pupil assessment.
	• Ensuring that the school's curriculum is fully effective.

At this stage, the critical success factors are not measured or measurable; they are purely an analysis of the job into its key elements. After clarifying the boundaries of the job, it is necessary to examine the environment in order to see what performance is required in these areas.

Stage Three – The SWOT analysis

The SWOT analysis is a well-known marketing process which is used to define priorities for a business, examining its own strengths and weaknesses in relation to its business and social environment. This should be seen in relation to the job that needs to be done and follows the stages of clarifying job purpose and job boundaries. An analysis of performance is only appropriate when there is a yardstick against which to make an analysis.

SWOT-ting is a useful way of evaluating current performance, comparing that against future obstacles and opportunities and using the information to generate a list of priorities for the manager and subordinate to discuss during the contracting process. The process hinges around several topics for discussion:

> What is the job holder doing well; what features of the job are exceeding normal performance requirements and how can we capitalise of these strengths even further?

Building on strengths is an easier process than removing limitations; it is normally a question of accelerating a rising trend and increasing momentum in a situation where forward movement is already apparent.

> What weaknesses are displayed by the job holder in relation to the agreed job? Are they critical to the execution of the whole job or can they be either dumped or improved upon?

Weaknesses must be relevant to the critical success factors in the job, otherwise they may create unnecessary conflict. If they are critical, then a clear action plan needs to be agreed to ensure that the weaknesses are removed.

> What things are happening in the future which may be supporting new initiatives? In what direction is the tide running and how can we launch our ships at the right time to catch it? What opportunities are available to enhance the job holder's performance? What do we need to do to capitalise on them?

Changes to the business operation can be seen as opportunities or threats. Opportunities are events which may help to move the business forward, possibly to exceed current performance targets.

> What future events may threaten our achievement of the performance contract and how might they be prevented? What contingencies do we need to develop to ensure that they do not compromise our business plans?

Threats or risks need to be managed. It is important to review possible threats to the business early so that preventative and contingent measures can be taken.

Stage Four – What do your customers expect?

The fourth stage and an important element of information gathering is to clarify the requirements and expectations of the job holder's customers.

The relationship between supplier and customer should be subject to the discipline of performance contracts in order to regularise it. Before clarifying individual performance contracts, managers should either agree contracts with their customers or have a clear idea of their expectations.

After the wave of TQM programmes, it almost goes without saying that the customer may be either internal or external. The front line staff who deal directly with the revenue-generating customer may not formalise a contract – although what an excellent marketing opportunity that can be – but they do need to know how to structure their proposition to the customer so that it meets the customer's expectations, and how the proposition compares with that of any competitors. Initially, customers need to be consulted and their views on performance requirements sought and codified. Performance contracts should cascade from top management to front line staff; they should also flow laterally from front line service or production staff back through support staff and other functions.

For example, a front line requirement in a finance house may be to put terminals in every car dealer's premises in order to meet a service objective of reducing processing time on car loans. This immediately creates a requirement for the IT department to have, say, 50 terminals in place by the end of the year to meet particular specifications. Effective, co-ordinated organisations have in place both a hierarchy *and* a network of performance contracts.

Stage Five – What are the main output requirements?

There are two main sets of performance requirements in a performance contract – output objectives and capability objectives.

The process of defining output objectives should use the information gained from the previous stages in order to state clearly what service levels are required for each critical success factor. This analysis is quite straightforward:

- For each critical success factor, list two or three important activities that are currently going on.
- In the light of your SWOT analysis and review of customer requirements, decide whether your current activities need to be:
  - Maintained at their current level
  - Improved
  - Dropped or delegated elsewhere in the organisation
- Decide whether new elements in each critical success factor need to be developed.

- Set clear and unambiguous measures for each of these activities, where possible in terms of output or, in some areas, in terms of outcome. It is important not to have too many outcome related objectives as these will focus too closely on only two or three indicators (sales, profit, labour turnover etc.) at the expense of putting in place activities which express the overall service performance of the job.
- These objectives should be measured where possible on the basis of quantity, quality, time and cost. This gives scope for the future to make improvements in all areas.
- It is important that the extra amount of output required in critical success factors should be balanced either by additional resources or by dropping other activities. Dropping an unnecessary activity is as important a decision as developing something new; it releases resources and energy for other projects.

Stage Six – Where do we need to improve in order to meet our service requirements?

Output targets don't achieve themselves; they are related to the requirements of today's customer and today's business. If they are to be achieved now and in the future, they need to be supported by a set of capability objectives. Quite simply, each objective in each critical success factor needs to be augmented by a capability objective which is equally measurable and unambiguous, to ensure that there is some mechanism for increasing the job holders capability for achieving the new service objective.

For example, the capability objective in an organisation which is moving from a production led to a marketing led strategy would need to ensure, as well as setting targets to ensure that service levels to customers were being increased, that their staff were competent to carry out good customer service and that the various customers' databases were enhanced by Information Technology staff and so on.

The reason for introducing capability objectives is to ensure that an appropriate infrastructure is set in place as a key part of the job – rather than, as in many performance management systems, setting short-term targets without any thought for the long term. Growth in capability is as important strategically in the long term as growth in current business performance. We have already seen that people cannot perform beyond their competence; neither can organisations perform beyond their capability. If your people, systems and structures are not as effective as your competitors, then all other things being equal, your capacity to perform will be lower.

The process of generating capability objectives is similar to generating output objectives. For each output objective you need to ask:

1. To achieve this objective, what do I need to do in terms of organisation structure, management processes, additional physical resources, systems or the competence of my people?
2. What do I need to improve? What capability factors must I maintain? What new elements must I develop? Can I drop or delegate some things in other sections in order to make room for the things I need to achieve?

The final set of performance requirements should look like Figure 6. Figure 7 shows how this matrix has been applied to set objectives for a manager in a multiple food retail business.

Critical success factor	Output objectives	Capability objectives
Key performance area 1	Objective: 1 2 3	Objective: 1 2 3
Key performance area 2	Objective: 1 2	Objective: 1 2
Key performance area 3	Objective: 1 2 3	Objective: 1 2 3

Figure 6 *Performance requirements matrix*

The aim of the performance contract is to give people a clear idea of the performance expected of them across the key elements of their job. Splitting performance requirements into output and capability objectives results in a change of emphasis at different levels within the organisation. The more strategic the job, the richer the mixture of objectives in favour of capability; a more operational role is more likely to have predominantly output objectives. Many organisations avoid the dichotomy altogether, preferring instead to focus on a mixture of measurable objectives without clarifying their output or capability focus.

Critical success factor	Output objectives	Capability objectives
1. *Development of the annual sales plan*	1.1 Achievement of the annual sales plan target of £300K per week 1.2 Carry out detailed review of local competitor activity	1.1 Training programme set up for management team on sales department 1.2 Organise merchandising review of fresh food area
2. *Containment of controllable costs*	2.1 Achievement of business plan – net controllable costs 2.2 Reduce energy costs by 5% in addition to plan	2.1 Set up staff communications programme on cost control 2.2 Arrange for improved roof insulation in warehouse
3. *Staff management and development*	3.1 Reduce labour turn over to 35% rolling year on year 3.2 Agree performance contracts with all management team 3.3 Agree training plan with district manager	3.1 Recruit new Personnel and Training Manager 3.2 Arrange for training from Personnel Department for all departments 3.3 Refurbish training room/review all training equipment
4. *Provision of customer service*	4.1 Achieve 'out of stock' target of 40 lines maximum by end January 4.2 Implement new company check-out scheduling 4.3 Arrange store visits by voluntary groups	4.1 Implement customer care Package 4.2 Arrange for bag packing training at checkouts 4.3 Agree incentive programme with staff council
5. *Control of wastage*	5.1 Achieve wastage level target of 4.1% for the year 5.2 Reduce stock levels in warehouse by £150K 5.3 Implement by end of year, company stock management system	5.1 Agree training package on new Food Handling Act 5.2 Re-write staff shopping policy
6. *Compliance with company systems and procedures*	6.1 Achieve 85% or more in all QA inspections 6.2 Review all in-store computer security – no unauthorised entries allowed 6.3 Adhere to all company standards as set out in the manager's policy guide	6.1 Ensure all procedural manuals are up-to-date and explained to staff 6.2 Re-structure top management team and clarify accountabilities for compliance 6.3 Conduct a hygiene and safety audit

Figure 7 *Retail manager: performance requirements*

6

Assessing the Support Requirements

Many performance management programmes stop at the agreement of performance requirements – an unsatisfactory state of affairs as it implies a one-sided contract with all the obligations on one side, that of the employee. Even organisations who use performance contracts as a basis for managing performance often fail to specify support requirements with quite the same clarity and detail as they set out the performance requirements. To have one side of the performance contract set out in clear and measurable terms, often in writing, whilst the other side is 'implied' and couched in vague and unmeasurable statements of intent, seems to me to be particularly unfair. If a performance contract is to be fully effective it needs to have two sides which are equally measurable and equally enforceable.

This is the essence of performance contracting: I expect from you 'x' units of output during the next year, in return I will give you 'y' units of support. Both of these sides of the contract should be reviewable during the performance review meeting and if it is relevant, both may be increased or decreased at that time. As a former personnel manager, I found that many of the performance problems occurring in organisations related to a deficiency in support rather than poor performance from the individual.

The member of staff requires an agreement of support in four key areas:

1. **Resources:** There should be agreement on the level of resources required and available to achieve the performance requirements.
2. **Training/personal development:** It is important for both parties to agree some important personal development objectives in order to enable the individual to achieve the performance requirements. The

development of competence is always going to be a necessary prerequisite of effective business performance.

3. **Authority:** Part of the role of the manager and an important element in effective delegation is the establishment of individual authority and the communication of that authority to all parties who need to know.

These three elements – resources, personal development and authority – are the essence of empowerment. When they are clearly defined and pitched at an appropriate level for the performance requirements of the job, the individual is fully empowered to achieve high performance. There is, however, a fourth issue:

4. **The amount of direction and support required from the manager:** What Hersey and Blanchard call 'contracting for leadership style'. This is the level of interaction that the individual should get from their manager and whether that interaction should be in the form of direction or support.

The contract is two-way and needs to be as clear and measurable in relation to the support requirements as it is to the performance requirements. This is important for two reasons – one rational, the other motivational. The rational reason is that, as we have already seen, we need to balance every improvement in output with an appropriate improvement in capability, this is because of the need to ensure both current and future performance is achieved. This is equally relevant in relation to the balance between the performance requirements and support requirements with the performance contract. If we try to get greater performance from an individual without increasing their personal or physical resources, then we are growing our business at the expense of our people rather than along with our people – like trying to run a car without oil or maintenance; sooner or later it will grind to a halt. Clarifying the support requirements helps to ensure that the individual's competence grows in line with the demands made of them; this should help to ensure that they are capable of achieving more in the future.

The opposite occurs when the individual's resources are stretched beyond breaking point when trying to achieve challenging goals with diminishing resources – often they become burnt-out and their confidence is broken by having to achieve the impossible without the necessary support, so that in the future demands are less likely to be achieved.

Each of the four support areas, resources, training/development, authority and leadership, is critical to the continued high performance of the individual. Without the necessary resources, the individual cannot meet *all* the performance requirements. They are only able to meet some of them, and at the expense of others – product quality, staff development, customer service and so on. Without the necessary training and development people cannot extend their level of competence and so their performance is limited. We have already seen that performance is constrained by the boundaries of individual competence; part of the performance contract must seek to bridge those gaps.

If there is a lack of authority, the individual cannot be held accountable for the achievement of their part of the performance contract. Authority and accountability balance each other out; in fact the organisation chart is full of invisible arrows which indicate the downward flow of authority balanced by the upward flow of accountability. The two concepts should be in equilibrium – people can only be fully accountable when they have full authority.

Finally, the agreement on leadership style is critical to the relationship between the two parties to the contract. It helps both parties to understand their level of commitment in terms of time and 'emotional' support.

The second reason for ensuring that these four factors are clearly stated is motivational. Performance management is as much about generating commitment and engaging real feelings as it is about the rational process of setting targets and measuring output. Often, as managers, we expect to get staff commitment on targets and deliverable output whilst failing to give any commitment ourselves in terms of support and resources.

The root of the two words professional and amateur tells us a lot. In my dictionary, professional comes from *profess*, to make a public confession (an original performance contract?) and goes on to talk about training, discipline and education. The word amateur, however, refers to people who do something literally for the love of the subject. In many organisations we use motivation to develop a sense of amateurism; we expect people to do things for the love of the company, loyalty to their boss or simply for the greater general good. Perhaps in many companies, some people feel a little like the soldier in the front line who is facing a frontal attack and has just fired his last bullet – there is not much left for the manager to do but to make one last appeal to their finer feelings.

Contracts are based on three elements – coercive, co-operative and calculative. We want to base our contracts on mutual co-operation but they also need to appeal to people's sense of self-interest. If there is a clear commitment to support, stated unequivocally and liable to the same review process as performance objectives, people are more likely to feel committed to achieving their side of the contract. Norman Dixon in his excellent book *On the Psychology of Military Incompetence* (Jonathan Cape, 1976), points out that the great and successful military leaders like

Wellington, Shaka the Zulu and Montgomery took immense pains to improve the welfare of their men, in direct contrast to the unsuccessful and inept British Generals of both the Crimea and Boer Wars where the armies were defeated as much by disease and logistical incompetence as by the enemy.

Effective support makes a sound base for improved performance. If resources are not available, then contracts need to be reviewed to ensure that those activities which need to be carried out can be carried out effectively. This is, however, not a recipe for profligacy – people need enough resources to meet their requirements; too many and the inputs start to outweigh the outputs – ineffective in terms of both cost and individual development.

The essence of support requirements is the clarification of levels of resources available, not vague promises of support. How this part of the contract is set out is now something to review in more detail.

RESOURCES

One of the most regular complaints which people have at work is that they lack the resources to do their particular job. We feel that if we only had more money, more equipment or more people we would do a more effective job. This lack of resources can be both a problem and an opportunity. It is a problem if the lack of resources is a barrier to high performance and good quality work; it is an opportunity when it makes people review their work in order to look for less resource-hungry solutions to their problems.

There are two prevalent solutions to resource shortages in many organisations – the shark who wants to grab as much as possible and the minnow who spends time swimming about in circles complaining how awful it is that the organisation won't spend more money on their department. Organisations need to agree some form of middle way, a way in which resources can be allocated to individuals as part of their performance contract in relation to their needs rather than their propensity to build empires.

Clearly, people need the resources – money, people, assets and time – to do the work that they are expected to do. Those four areas need to be kept in balance and are often interchangeable. We may decide to swap people for machinery by automating some elements of our job; we may decide to exchange people for money by sub-contracting, and so on. We do, however, have to ensure that:

- resources are allocated in relation to the performance requirements of the division, department and individual. Any less will make it difficult to achieve the whole performance contract;

- those resources need to be sufficient to achieve those requirements but no more. Excess resources, unless they can be converted into additional output, do little for the organisation and should be transferred to an area that has greater resource requirements;
- the blend of resources needs to be the most efficient mixture of people, time, money and machinery that can be devised. If people resources are a problem, we should be looking for the most effective alternative;
- sudden resource crises caused by government policy or financial catastrophes should not be met by 'across the board' type cuts; the cuts should still be made in relation to performance requirements – the people being asked to do more in a crisis should not be cut as much as those whose requirements remain unchanged.

There are two mechanisms which help us to carry out our review of resources – zero based budgeting and the performance contract.

Zero based budgeting

This is the process of starting the budget process from a zero base rather than basing it on last year's figures. Each cost then has to be justified in its own right rather than on the basis of previous figures plus inflation and a little bit more. Accountants recommend it when it appears that there is more fat than meat in the budget. I believe it is useful for the first performance contract discussion and, perhaps, biannually after that. It is too lengthy a process to be used every year but too important a process not to be used at all, and is particularly effective if used in conjunction with *'bench-marking'*, that is examining resources in relation to other effective organisations with a similar market base. It may not always prevent the sharks getting a disproportionate share of resources but it does make them justify their share on a regular basis. Zero based budgeting is a powerful tool particularly when harnessed to an effective performance contracting process.

The performance contract

This has two sets of performance requirements – output and capability objectives. The manager who is concerned to see resources growing should review the capability objectives to encourage their people to work on producing more with less but in a way that retains high standards in other parts of the operation. This is one of the strengths of contracting for performance across the whole job. In traditionally run organisations, resource-pressure is met by rapid cost cutting and targets are produced to ensure that these costs *are* cut. This is done at the expense of other critical success factors – like staff development and product quality. It is important that continuous work is done to squeeze excessive costs from the business incrementally as part of the whole job and not in huge swathes in response to the immediate pressure of events.

TRAINING AND PERSONAL DEVELOPMENT

Organisations need to focus continually on improving their infrastructure – people and assets. The most critical of these is the ongoing development of people. This is a key part of the support that everyone in an organisation needs from their manager. Development needs to be constant and incremental in contrast to the old style focus of training and development relating only to promotion. Promotion is the step change which occurs when somebody moves up from one job to another or from one grade to another. Traditionally it has been the focus for performance appraisal and the assessment of potential. The concept of on-going promotion is an anachronistic throwback to the pyramidal multi-layered organisations of the past, where a manager could expect several promotions during his or her career.

In contrast, continuous development is the process by which people develop new skills and learn new things so that they develop incrementally over a period of time. In most careers there will be, however, one or two step changes where promotions occur, but promotions are less common now and should be seen as part of overall staff development. Continuous development is, therefore, the gradual and continuous accumulation of competency throughout the whole career.

Continuous development depends on the interplay between three factors – the organisation, the manager and the individual. Ideally, much of the management of continuous development should be generated by the individual themselves. The manager, however, stands in relation to the individual as the parent to the child. By setting targets, providing feedback and carrying out effective performance reviews, the manager gives guidance to the individual and can help to shape their development. In addition, the organisation has a responsibility to create an environment in which individuals can develop and also to focus their development in a direction which will support the organisation's strategy in the future. We will examine this in future chapters.

Perhaps the most important concept relating to continuous development is that of learning. Learning implies adaption to the environment. It is the concept which supports evolutionary change. The organisation must ensure that its rate of learning is equal to or greater than the rate of change in its external environment. If the organisation and the people within it are unable to learn and develop in order to keep pace with the performance required of them in their working environment, then it will eventually suffer the fate of all extinct animals. I recently ran, with a colleague, a development programme for consultants in the National Health Service, who were having to change their work style in order to adapt to the changes in relation to the NHS internal market. They suddenly found themselves needing to acquire skills and knowledge which previously had not been necessary. However, the acquisition of these skills was critical to the survival of both them and their organisation's effectiveness. They were learning that adaption to change is a key part of *any* organisation's function: to be aware of the changes taking place in the world outside and converting those into objectives for people inside the organisation.

A further issue in the continuous development of people is that people learn the most within their normal work situation. Douglas McGregor in *The Human Side of Enterprise* (McGraw-Hill, 1960) made the following observation:

> the day by day experience at work is so much more powerful that it tends to overshadow what the individual may learn in other settings.

Work is full of learning opportunities if they are perceived and identified by the individual.

This concept of workplace learning is connected with the role of the manager as trainer and coach. Managers cannot help teaching their staff, in the same way as a parent cannot help but teach their children. Douglas McGregor has said:

> every encounter between a superior and a subordinate involves learning of some kind for the subordinate (it should involve learning for the superior too, but that is another matter).

Managers teach the people who work for them because they set targets, give feedback, reprimand and praise and, by so doing, they set the environment in which the individual is working and, therefore, the environment to which the individual needs to adapt. Managing the performance and development of the individual is a critical success factor for every manager. Unfortunately, it is too often a catch-all paragraph at the end of a job description, and is also one of the areas in which managers themselves are set very few standards or targets.

Continuous development is a concept which applies throughout the organisation, not simply for a few key managers and professionals at the top of the hierarchy; in fact it is probably even more important for those people working in the 'front line'. In the same way, continuous development should apply throughout the whole of an individual's career. There is a view held by organisations (and individuals within them) that training and development is strictly for the young. Young people are often, if they are lucky, the recipients of large chunks of training and development during the first few years of their working life. This intellectual indigestion is balanced out by a complete dearth of formal training and development activities for the remainder of their career. Whilst training and development is important for young people in organisations, nevertheless it is equally important for people to continue to be developed until they leave the organisation. Development does not stop at 40! The reason for this anachronistic view goes back to the idea of development equalling promotion. Many people held the view that they only received training and development in order to help them gain promotion to the next level within the organisation. Once that promotion ladder had been cut off and they became what was known as a 'plateaued manager' their interest in development ceased, and they preferred to carry on working in their established pattern. This is clearly an unsatisfactory view in a world where managers and staff need to learn hard in order to survive.

To ensure that an individual's rate of learning is at least equivalent to their performance requirements, the manager needs to carry out the following processes:

- A 'zero-based' assessment of competence in relation to the performance required of the individual.
- An action plan to fill any competence gaps.
- Discussion with training and development professionals on appropriate training solutions to help fulfil any identified competence gaps.
- A review of the manager's own coaching style in relation to the individual and the level of direction and support required.

DIRECTION AND SUPPORT

Training and development is the joint responsibility of the individual and manager and those responsibilities need to be encapsulated in the performance contract. Another important issue in their relationship is the manager's leadership style in relation to the individual. Important work on this has been done by Paul Hersey and Ken Blanchard in their academic work *Management of Organisational Behaviour* and the more popular *Leadership and the One Minute Manager* by Ken Blanchard, Patricia and Drea Zigarmi.

The essence of situational leadership is that normally if you ask a manager to describe their management style, the reply will probably be couched in quite specific terms – 'I'm an autocrat' or 'I like to give my people some space' or 'I see myself as a coach'. The answer should be 'It depends, it depends on ... what my people need, how experienced a team I have, what situation we are in' and so on. Managers should take into account the competence and the commitment of their people and before deciding how much direction to give in terms of clear guidance on performance requirements and process, and how much support they need to carry out the job. These two elements come together to produce four effective leadership styles:

1. Directing – The manager concentrates on giving clear direction, explaining what to do and how to do it, in fairly concrete terms. This style is appropriate for people who are inexperienced in particular aspects of their work and who need to develop competence.
2. Coaching – When coaching, the manager continues to give clear direction but begins to give people more scope, perhaps in the form of a longer period between performance reviews or less direction on the work method or, perhaps, by asking the individual to recommend action for the manager's agreement. This is an appropriate style for people who are still learning their job and beginning to develop the confidence to do their job in their own way.
3. Supporting – This is the first stage where a manager practises a more 'hands-off' style – setting objectives and then leaving the individual to identify work methods for themselves, giving 'moral' support where necessary in order to build up confidence. This style is appropriate for competent people who, either through lack of confidence or lack of motivation, are not working to their full potential.
4. Delegating – This is the stage where the manager sets clear objectives and then sits back, allowing the individual high levels of discretion with the occasional performance review. This is appropriate for competent people with the confidence and motivation to work on their own.

These four styles are effective when they are applied appropriately. The highly competent person would be aggrieved to be managed in a directive style; in the same way the inexperienced learner would feel vulnerable and unsupported to be managed in the delegative style. It is important to identify an individual's development level for each critical success factor and then manage them in that area in an appropriate style. It is also appropriate to agree exactly what that style should be, otherwise it may be misconstrued as either over- or under-managing in relation to other members of the team who will have different needs.

Management styles can be compared to the gearing of a motor vehicle. First gear (directive) is a good starter gear but unlikely to generate much movement or speed. Second gear (coaching) is where there is greater movement with less management effort and so on until fourth gear (directive) where there is both movement and speed with the minimum of management effort. Staff should be moved up gear by gear and managers should not make major changes to the agreed approach, but instead decreasing the amount of direction as the individual shows signs of development. This incrementalism is equally appropriate when performance drops off; the manager should give a little more support and direction, moving down the gears, as it were.

The key questions a manager should be asking in relation to each critical success factor are:

- How competent is the individual to meet the performance requirements?
- How confident are they and how committed?
- How much direction do they need?
- How much support and morale boosting is needed?

There are two management styles at either end of the scale which must be avoided at all costs – **dictating** – giving the individual no discretion at all – and **abdicating** – giving them too much discretion and leaving them to 'get on with it' alone. Even the best staff need some interaction with their boss, otherwise their work may go off track.

AUTHORITY

Accountability is an important concept underpinning the performance cycle. It literally means the things that people are held to account for. If an organisation is to be fully effective and the people within it to perform well, then it is important that the whole organisation is based on a clear system of accountability, ie everyone knowing what they are responsible for and to whom they are responsible.

The concept of accountability goes hand in hand with that of authority. Authority is the legitimate use of power within an organisation – the basis upon which individuals operate and have influence. The relationship between authority and accountability can be defined very clearly by looking at an organisation chart. When we follow the line of an organisation chart downwards, we are looking at the authority relationships and when we trace those lines upwards, we are looking at the concept of accountability. That is an important concept. It is wrong for us to give someone authority without making them accountable for its use and, conversely, it is wrong to make someone accountable for something if they do not have the authority to influence.

An example of this is a foreman, held responsible for the performance of his workers without the authority to discipline them. A more complicated example may be related to profit responsibility. Many job descriptions say that unit managers, eg retail store managers, are responsible for achieving sales and profit objectives within their store. However, closer examination of their accountability normally leads us to the conclusion that they are, in fact, not fully accountable for all the components of bottom line profit and yet often they are judged purely on their contribution to that indicator, even though they may not have the authority to set prices, change merchandising plans or even agree the store layout.

Authority in its organisational sense is called *structural authority*. The only way to gain more structural authority is to gain promotion or to increase formal authority over resources. This is normally clarified in the job description – which should specify levels and limits of authority. However, there are other ways of using and gaining authority. Within a large organisation, senior line managers will have significant structural authority and be seen as powerful people. But there are several other types of authority which managers and staff possess which also create their own accountability. For example, expert authority is spread more evenly throughout the organisation than structural authority. Everyone within the organisation has some expert authority, even if it is only a more detailed understanding of their own job than anyone else. This is becoming more important as jobs change rapidly with the introduction of new systems and new technology. People who did a specific job four or five years ago and have subsequently been promoted may actually have lost touch with the way it is done now; the person who is actually doing the job will be seen as the leading authority. That means they become accountable for the application of that knowledge. It also means that their boss should recognise that authority in the performance contract and support it with the necessary formal authority.

Under these circumstances, we begin to understand how accountability works. The manager who has structural authority has responsibility to use it as effectively as possible to support and direct the 'expert' authority of the people who work for him. This is a key part of the process of organisational devolution. When organisations decentralise they devolve authority to a lower level within the organisation. The logic of this is that the lower level is better able to use its expert authority because of its proximity to either the customer, the market or the geographic region. When that authority is devolved, then an appropriate upward accountability must be registered.

As a rule it is important to ensure that authority is devolved to the lowest possible level within the organisation – an important factor in the concept of empowerment. People who are given the authority to act cannot help but accept accountability. People who are accountable for something *must* be given the authority to exercise that accountability. These two factors ensure that people take responsibility for their own actions and their own areas of operation.

As part of the performance contract, managers need to ensure the following:

- that the individual knows what they are accountable for and that all aspects of the performance requirements are things that they can influence (in the modern complex organisation, they may not have overall influence on many things; there is a strong element of shared accountability. For example, who is accountable for labour turnover, the general manager or the personnel manager? The answer is both – they each have accountabilities which impact on the labour turnover figures. These accountabilities will appear in both their performance contracts and labour turnover may be a output objective for both people. The hope is that this will encourage them to work together to bring the turnover figure down).
- Ensure that a clear statement of authority is included in their performance contract so that they are completely sure that they have the authority to do what they are required to do. If they don't have complete authority, the contract needs to clarify whose agreement they need in order to meet those objectives.

These four support requirements of the performance contract, resources, training, authority and leadership, are critical to the effective execution of the other half of the contract – the performance requirements. The next chapter reviews how the whole contract comes together.

7

The Performance Contract

The most difficult performance contract to draw up is the first one. Subsequent review discussions tend to amend the contract rather than substantially transform it, although it is advisable to zero-base the whole contract every year or two, by saying 'how would we tackle this job if we were coming to it afresh?' Setting up the initial performance contract is quite time consuming and requires research and reflection. It does, however, become easier with time and practice. It is a similar process to business planning and budgeting – and how many of us have found that difficult when we have come to it for the first time? In this chapter I have set out a suggested agenda for an initial performance contract process – not as a compulsory programme chiselled in stone but as a useful thought starter.

One of the most difficult issues which arises, particularly for managers who are not familiar with the process of setting performance objectives, is the fairness of the objectives. Within the concept of performance contracting is an underlying mutual dependency between manager and subordinate. The contracting process should be cascaded from the top of the organisation, so that managers have an incentive to agree staff targets that are achievable, otherwise if a member of their team fails to meet their objectives, then so will their manager. This will happen if the objectives are too easy *or* too difficult.

The solution to this is mutual interest. The best of all possible worlds is the manager and all his subordinates achieving their performance requirements. In order for this to happen, the following conditions need to be met:

- The performance requirements for each individual should reflect accurately the performance requirements of the manager. This does not mean that the manager should distribute *all* of his objectives to his subordinates – this would raise a question mark against the validity of the senior role. There are certain critical success factors, staff development for example, which should not be delegated. The performance requirements for each individual should be challenging enough to ensure that the manager's contract will also be achieved, but not so tough that they become unachievable. In the 'too tough' scenario both parties lose because they both fail to make their contract.

- The support requirements in each contract should balance the performance requirements, so that people are not being asked to do work without the appropriate levels of support. Again, it is in the manager's interest to ensure that their subordinates succeed.
- There needs to be consistency across performance requirements for the whole team, whereby all contracts are mutually supportive. This does not mean standardisation – every individual contract will differ in some way. Performance contracts can have a significant impact on bringing the team together, particularly as the achievements of all the manager's own performance requirements make it imperative to have an effective working team pulling together behind a clear set of objectives. Performance contracts should be publishable, so that team members know what objectives their colleagues are working towards. This can be an effective agenda for team meetings.

One further mechanism which helps to balance out performance demands across the organisation is the introduction of customer/supplier performance contracts, covered in more detail in Chapter 11. These *lateral performance contracts* have an important influence on the manager/subordinate requirements because they focus on the service objectives for other parts of the organisation. In some of the more specialised departments, the service objectives will probably be driven as much by the needs of other line managers as by their functional boss. Those performance requirements will normally be a balance between supporting the strategy line departments and maintaining professional standards.

Performance contracts provide the basis for many of the other processes which relate to appraisal and reward. It is important that the process of contracting is established before it becomes too closely associated with remuneration – mainly because the process, when approached for the first time, is difficult enough without adding the complication of possible financial gain or loss. Establish the contracting process first in order to avoid turning the first performance contract discussion into a pay negotiation which, rather than enhancing the performance management process, is likely to detract from it.

The development of the contract will vary with the experience of the two parties. Rather in line with the situational leadership model, the less experienced subordinate should have the performance contract set for them; experienced people should be asked to put together their own proposals for the contract and have them agreed by their boss. This extends situational leadership to contracting by recognising that people with greater experience can and should take greater responsibility for their own performance.

The final issue with regard to the contract is the setting of the review date. Here there are several factors which need to be taken into account. The first is the rate of change in the business. In a fast changing business, reviewing the performance contract needs to be more frequent to ensure that any off-track performance is spotted early before it becomes a major issue. It also creates more confidence if people are given regular, objective feedback on their performance, particularly if they are working in unknown areas. Secondly, the less experienced subordinate will require more regular reviews of their performance contract in order to keep a closer control on their progress.

The following notes set out the whole of the contracting process in the form of an agenda:

AGENDA FOR CHANGE – setting up a performance contract meeting

Setting up the performance contract is not a trivial process that can be carried out in one short meeting to keep the personnel department happy. The objective of the performance contract is to direct and manage individual performance for a significant period with consequences well beyond that. It is the *key* process in the relationship between manager and subordinate and, as such, it is important that it is carried out effectively with due care and attention. The length of the process depends on the complexity of the job and the level of experience of both manager and subordinate. There are, however, a number of stages which need to be worked through.

Stage One – Agreeing the purpose and structure of the job

The first stage is for both parties to agree exactly what the job is and what the critical success factors are. This is important to gain some joint agreement at an early stage so that both parties can carry out research on the needs of customers with a measure of consensus on the nature and boundaries of the job. This process may need to be revised if market research reveals additional critical success factors that should be taken into account, but the whole of the contracting process is likely to be iterative at the first attempt. The main questions that need to be asked at this stage are:

- Why does the job exist? What would *not* happen if the job disappeared?
- What are the main strategic outcomes that this job is responsible for producing? What is the job holder's responsibility for profit, sales, cost containment, labour turnover, stock levels and so on? What are the likely global measures of the job holder's success?
- What does the manager expect the job holder to do? How does this relate to customers served by the organisation?
- What are the critical success factors in the job? What are the core responsibilities to produce output for other people? What are the really critical mistakes that the job holder can make in the job? (critical mistakes are often the indicators of where the core of the job lies – if you want to find these out, ask the job holder what they can do to really mess up their job!)

The outcome of this stage should be agreement between manager and subordinate on the main purpose of the job and the critical success factors.

Stage Two – Market research

The next stage should be undertaken individually by both parties to several internal and external customers, preferably those who use the service most and those who are most open and eloquent in their criticism of the service that you offer. In almost every organisation in which I have worked as a personnel manager there has always been one key line manager who has been regarded as the scourge of the personnel department. I have always gone directly to them when trying to analyse my own function's performance – I have also gone to other managers with a more positive viewpoint, as much to boost my flagging morale after a discussion with the 'scourge' as to balance out the picture of strengths and weaknesses! Typical questions I would ask included:

- What type of service are you looking for from my department?
- What elements of that service do we do well?
- Where can we improve?
- How do you see your needs changing in the future?
- What have we introduced that you regard as unnecessary?
- What additional services would you like to see us develop?

Both manager and subordinate should tackle these questions at their respective levels. Service may differ in quality from the strategic picture to the delivery of the service on the ground. You may wish to capture this by encouraging dialogue between functions at all levels in the organisation and ensuring that the information is fed into the performance contracting process.

Stage Three – Analysis of results

The second meeting between manager and individual should be to analyse the results of the market research. Essentially, the meeting should consist of two stages:

1. Draft up a SWOT analysis (strengths, weaknesses, opportunities and threats), preferably on a flip chart so that there is a common reference point. The questions we should ask for each critical success factor are:
   a) Where do we meet or exceed the expectations of our customers?
   b) How can we capitalise on this to develop new services or improve even further the ones we are currently delivering?
   c) Where do we fail to meet the expectations of our customers?
   d) What must we do to improve?
   e) What events during the next few months or years do we need to prepare for?
   f) Which of those are positive and likely to help us to achieve our goals?
   g) What barriers exist which may prevent us from achieving those goals?
2. Review each of our main relationships in the organisation and try to assess what they will look for from us and our team. We need to look at them from the following angles:
   a) What service(s) to them do we need to improve?
   b) What new service(s) do we need to develop?
   c) What can we maintain at our current level?
   d) What services should be dropped (what do we do that they don't need)?

Stage Four – Setting the contract

The first stage of this process is to confirm that critical success factors – after a programme of research – still stand as valid reflections of the core of the job. If they don't, what other critical success factors should be added? Remember that critical success factors are not objectives; they are only a way of breaking the whole job up into the critical areas in which high performance is required.

For each critical success factor, the following questions need to be answered:

- What are the main objectives which need to be achieved in order to increase our level of service in this area? What needs to be improved, what new service needs to be developed, what service should we maintain?
- How will we measure our success in these objectives?
- What will we need to do better in order to achieve these objectives – a better use of assets, new systems, better trained people or organisational restructuring?
- How will we measure our success in these objectives?
- What resources will we need to meet both our output and capability objectives – equipment, money, people, time?
- What training will be required in order to achieve these performance requirements? What coaching will be necessary – does the manager need to give high or low levels of direction?
- Does the job holder have sufficient authority to enable him/her to meet the objectives? If so, what additional authority do they need? Who needs to know about it?

This process needs to be worked through for every critical success factor until a full performance contract – consisting of both performance and support requirements – has been agreed.

The next question is to agree the first review date and to summarise the performance contract *in writing* as a guidance document for both parties to direct future work. The performance contract should be a dynamic document, changing to meet the changing requirements of the business.

It has to be said that this is the 'gold-plated' version of the process, the one most likely to be used with professional or managerial staff. The process can be simplified for staff with more basic job aspirations or whose job has a clear set of measurable outputs which are unlikely to change. It is important, however, to set them some clear output and capability objectives – asking them how they feel they can improve their working methods, for example, and building that into the performance contract.

In my view and experience, the performance contract is valid at all levels.

8

Reviewing Performance

The key to effective management of performance is to have a set of processes within the organisation to ensure that contracts are fulfilled and uprated and that people within the organisation are developing fully in line with the current and future needs of the organisation.

Currently much of the responsibility for this falls on the performance appraisal system which is seen as a catch-all process for everything – managing performance, planning careers, giving feedback, assessing potential and deciding salary reviews. Regrettably the system cannot cope with this heavy responsibility and increasingly has come under pressure as an ineffective method of managing the range of issues that are subsumed under the performance management heading.

PROBLEMS RELATED TO THE 'TRADITIONAL' PERFORMANCE APPRAISAL APPROACH

Appraisal as confrontation

If the appraisal is an effective performance management process in which people can enhance their personal development and their contribution to the business, one must ask why it is approached by both parties with all the enthusiasm of a French aristocrat inspecting a guillotine. The appraisal is often seen as a showdown, a good sorting out or a clearing of the air. It is one of the tragedies of organisational life that an event with the most potential for good creates such ill-feeling. The reasons for this dysfunctional conflict are clear:

- lack of agreement on levels of performance;
- subjective feedback on performance ineffectively delivered;

- appraisals based on yesterday's performance and not on the whole year;
- disagreement on long-term career prospects.

An effective performance management process should address these issues in order to ensure that the business and the individuals move forward in partnership rather than hover around in ever-decreasing circles of conflict and disagreement.

Appraisal as judgement

One of the reasons for conflict in the appraisal is that it is seen as a one-sided process in which the manager acts as judge, jury and counsel for the prosecution. The process of performance management, if it is to be effective, needs to be jointly operated in order to retain the commitment and develop the self-awareness of the individual. Situational leadership and the other contingency theories of management and leadership tell us that managers should be slowly letting go of their directing roles and moving into a more supportive role as their staff become more experienced. This also relates to performance management, where there should be moves from supervisor to supporter over a period of time, thus enabling the individual to participate in the management of their own performance.

Appraisal as chat

The other extreme to be avoided is the 'chat around the coffee table' without either purpose or outcome. Performance management is a disciplined, structured process with clear objectives and joint ownership of any outcomes. Many managers, embarrassed by the need to give feedback and set stretching targets, reduce the appraisal to a few mumbled 'well dones!' and leave the interview with a briefcase full of unresolved issues that they have felt ill-equipped to raise.

Appraisal as bureaucracy

Many organisations have a complex and highly structured appraisal process, which has made it something to be got through as expeditiously as possible. It becomes a bureaucratic exercise, measured by the completion of the appropriate documentation. This approach is underpinned by a failure to understand the relevance of appraisal to both the manager and subordinate, as well as the organisation. The management of performance is not something introduced by and for the personnel department, it is a key process for the whole organisation – as critical as putting together the company's budget.

Appraisal as unfinished business

Appraisals should not be a one-off event. They should be and are part of an ongoing cycle of performance management.

Appraisal as annual event

A Distributive Industry Training Board video on appraisal was called 'The Annual Ordeal' – a richly evocative title for many people. In the current climate, to review performance once a year is ludicrously relaxed and undisciplined. Most targets set at appraisal become irrelevant and out of date within months or even weeks. Twelve months later both parties can hardly remember what was agreed and the whole process becomes a painful exercise in retrospective rationalisation rather than a stimulating exercise in forward thinking. Performance needs to be reviewed constantly in order to ensure that targets are relevant and being managed accurately.

REQUIREMENTS OF THE PERFORMANCE APPRAISAL PROCESS

There are several sets of requirements for meaningful performance appraisal. The organisation has certain needs, the managers within the organisation have certain needs, as do the individuals who work for them.

The prime motivation for performance management is for the individual. The individual needs to know how he or she is performing – this need can be fulfilled at two levels; a) the most effective; timely feedback, delivered on the job in a constructive format by someone they can trust, and b) the more formal review – to take the performance contract and review the whole job periodically. This review is, in my view, too important to leave until the personnel department decide to carry out the annual appraisal exercise and should be carried out either monthly or quarterly. This should be a full scale review of the performance contract in which both parties to the contract review their performance and take the opportunity to turn performance requirements up a notch in order to enhance the overall performance and to ensure that the support requirements are still appropriate.

The information from these performance reviews can then go further towards the 'annual' performance appraisal which becomes a development review to appraise the individual's progression in terms of personal development. For all three of these processes, both individual and manager are the main beneficiaries. The organisation receives its reward in terms of improved performance and enhanced contribution, but the processes are between two parties and the organisation's role is to facilitate the process by the provision of supporting documentation and management training. The process may relate to other systems within the organisation – primarily remuneration and benefits – but at this stage it is still effectively a contract between two people and primarily the issues raised at review are between them.

The annual development review, however, leads into a range of other performance management processes in which the organisation takes a more active interest. At this stage, it may be useful to compare the process of managing individual performance with the process of managing organisational performance.

Feedback is given to organisations every day by their customers; the organisation needs to review its performance regularly against the whole offer which it gives to its customers. It does not just review its sales and profit budget; an effective organisation takes regular measures of customer service, new product development, standards of product quality and so on, and compares them with customers' needs and competitor activity.

The development review has its corporate equivalent in the process of deriving strategic objectives. We have already seen that the SWOT analysis is as relevant to individuals as it is to their organisation. The development review is effectively an analysis of strengths and weaknesses in relation to the job that the individual is doing. The discussion leads onto opportunities and threats to review changes that are likely to take place and prepares plans to ensure that those changes can be managed by the individual.

Two principal things come out of these development reviews, as they do from their organisational equivalent – a review of current capability (training and development needs), and a discussion of strategic direction (career planning). The development review leads to several other processes. It answers the questions 'in what direction should I be developing for the future?' (career planning) and 'what training and development do I need to enhance my capacity to do my current job?'. Both of these issues need to be dealt with by other people within the organisation. Although the initial diagnosis needs to be made jointly between manager and staff, the resolution of questions of long-term career development needs an organisational perspective.

If career planning was a simple extrapolation of current progress, it would be easier to review between manager and staff. For many that may be an important part of the career development process and can be resolved internally. It does, however, require external advice on two issues. Firstly, the strategic direction of business (it is wrong to encourage people to develop their career in a direction which may run counter to the direction of the business). Secondly, a comparison of the competence of the individual with other potential competitors for progression within the organisation.

These issues combine career/development planning with the assessment of potential, the latter of which is a key process for individuals, managers and the organisation as a whole. It needs to be objective, with clear statements of standards required so that not only the organisation can make judgements, but individuals can understand how they can measure their potential against the future competence requirements of the business. Potential cannot be judged solely by a manager and subordinate working together; it is a strategic responsibility which requires an understanding of the future direction of the business and the skills and abilities required at each level of the organisation.

It is also difficult for a manager to assess the potential of her people beyond her own level. She may fail to spot high potential because of her own limitations and short-sightedness and may choose to interpret, for example, high levels of creative thinking as ineffective, blue-sky thinking – or sheer bloody-mindedness!

An effective method of assessment of potential, such as an assessment or development centre, should lead on to two further performance management processes – *succession planning* and *manpower planning*. The former is a detailed process of putting individual names against jobs for the future, the latter a quantitative and qualitative view of the numbers and type of people that the organisation will require in the future. Both processes are strategic and must be managed by the organisation as a whole, with the information fed back into the career plans and appraisals of people within the organisation.

PERFORMANCE MANAGEMENT PROCESSES

There are two trends for performance management processes:

- Informal (personal needs) to formal (organisational needs)
- Short-term (subjective) to long-term (objective)

Each process within these trends can be placed on a continuum (see Figure 8). We shall now look at these in more detail.

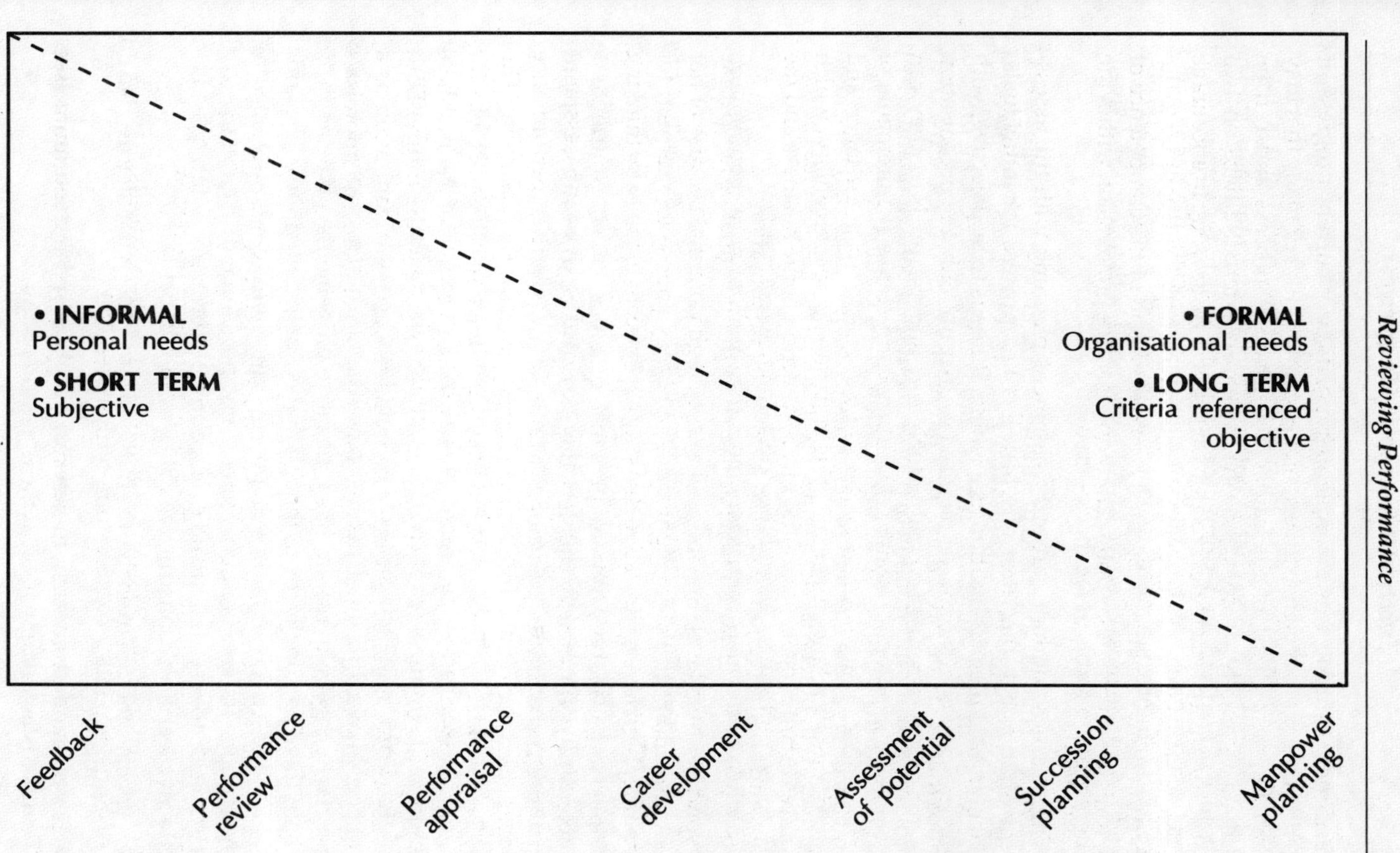

Figure 8 *Performance management – trends and processes*

Feedback

Feedback is the most effective form of performance review if it is timely and delivered in a form that is both instructive and motivational. The absence of feedback on performance is demotivating to the employee and creates a learning vacuum. Once managers appreciate the need to give feedback, they then need to learn to give both positive and critical feedback in the most effective way. People need both to learn effectively. There are two forms of feedback – crediting and criticising.

Crediting This is the skill of giving recognition to people whose performance helps the organisation meet its objectives. People work harder when their efforts are noticed and commended. Giving praise is more than a vague 'well done' or a pat on the back. An effective credit provides specific information to people about their behaviour and why it is creditworthy. This specific information gives credibility to the praise and encourages the element of performance to be repeated. It should not be overused, otherwise it becomes devalued. Generally it should be used:

- when performers exceed their performance requirements;
- when performers *consistently* meet their performance requirements; and
- when a performer achieves a level of performance *not usually met by that person*.

Credit can also be given to personal qualities which contribute to successful performance; this lets the individual know which personal qualities and attitudes are valued.

Constructive criticism This is necessary when people underperform on agreed performance requirements. The manager's role is to help them improve. Here the skill of criticism is to do this constructively, helping staff to learn from their mistakes without losing confidence.

People have difficulty listening to criticism. When someone's work is criticised, they may respond as if negative judgements are being made about them personally, even though that is not the intention of the critic.

Effective criticism improves poor performance without impairing motivation. Its aim is improvement, not punishment. Aggressive criticism leads to resentment and even poorer performance; it rarely leads to effective learning. Constructive criticism should be:

- specific enough to enable the individual to know what they need to do to improve;
- even-handed enough to refer to what is satisfactory as well as unsatisfactory;

- seeking solutions not scapegoats; those solutions should be jointly agreed.

Feedback is on-going, it should be delivered in the most positive way when a situation arises. It is, however, specific rather than wide-ranging, and needs to be done in a more formal way – by a performance review of the whole job.

Performance review

The purpose of performance review is to monitor and evaluate both elements of the performance contract. It is a simple process of reviewing the performance requirements for the whole job on the one hand, and on the other, reviewing the support requirements required by the job holder. The end of this chapter sets out agendas for the performance review discussion. In order to clarify the performance review process, I refer to the main topics of this below:

- A review of performance requirements achieved by the individual across the full range of critical success factors.
- A re-setting of targets when the performance contract is being met satisfactorily.
- A review of problems where the performance contract is not being met and the agreeing of an action plan to resolve them.
- A review of the manager's management style and an exploration of where work can be delegated further to the subordinate.
- Identification of training needs and, where appropriate, increased resources.

In order to conduct an effective performance review, several support systems need to be introduced and some barriers need to be removed (see Table 3).

Table 3 *Conducting an effective performance review*

Support systems	**Barriers**
• Clear and measurable performance requirements	• Vague and ambiguous performance requirements
• Effective management information systems to which both parties have access	• Information systems which are either too slow to generate information or have access restricted to senior managers
• Effective bespoke training programmes run by a responsive training section	• An inflexible menu of set training programmes with long lead times for attendance
• Reward systems based on objective measures of performance	• No connection between reward and performance.

Development discussion

The information generated by the performance review process is the key to successful management of performance. It is a constant cycle of target setting, review and re-setting, hopefully on an upward spiral of continuous improvement. This is analogous with the organisation's process of business planning and budgeting. However, there is a need for the individual, as with the organisation, to review their position in the market and look far ahead to ensure that they are moving in the right direction and that they are capable of making the appropriate moves.

The development discussion is the individual equivalent of the organisation's strategic plan and, as such, is an entirely separate exercise from the performance review (see Table 4).

Table 4 *Differences between performance review and development discussion*

Performance review	Development discussion
• Focused on the job	• Focused on the individual
• Manager led	• Joint discussion
• Review of results against targets	• Review of competency against future needs
• On-going performance	• Future development
• Performance based	• Competence based
• Analytical	• Predictive
• Reward-driven	• Career-driven
• Continuous improvement of the business	• Continuous development of the individual

Development discussions have changed in their nature because of the changing nature of commercial organisations. Confusing performance with development in human resource management is as dangerous as an organisation feeling confident because it continues to meet its budget whilst failing to address long-term issues of research, development and marketing strategy. Effective management of performance monitors today's performance whilst setting in motion the processes which will ensure effective performance for tomorrow and beyond.

There are important philosophical implications underpinning the development discussion. Development is a personal issue as well as an organisational one. Managers need to equip people to manage their own development and the nature of development discussions should take that into account. It is not merely an abdication of responsibility for individual career development on the manager's part. It is a gradual process in which the manager encourages the transfer of responsibility for their career management to the individual.

With inexperienced staff, the manager needs to provide strong career direction. This directive approach is tempered by an effective questioning technique to start the individual thinking about their career and development for themselves. With time, the manager can provide less direction and encourage more personal thinking until the process of reviewing person competence and future development planning becomes almost the total responsibility of what has become a mature and experienced employee.

Effective development discussions focus on the skill and knowledge required to be fully competent in the job – as it is and as it will become. The most effective development discussions begin with a clear and joint understanding of the skills, knowledge and attitudes which underpin the role, with the addition of any new competences that are likely to be required in order to achieve future business plans. A more detailed agenda for a development discussion is set out on page 106.

The key to effective performance review meetings and development discussions is skilled interviewing. Whilst the scope of the book does not demand a detailed review of these skills, the following notes may act as a refresher. They will also help to put into perspective the role of good interpersonal skills in relation to performance management. Well designed systems need to be operated by skilled and mature managers if they are to be fully effective. The key skills are questioning, listening and developing rapport.

Questioning Some television interviewers quite often ask a two or three minute question which can be answered in seconds by one or a few words. You end up knowing more about the questioner's attitude, beliefs and values that those of the person being interviewed. Conversely, the politician, by saying 'Before I answer that, let me just say ....', can deal with the question they wanted to answer rather than the question the interviewer asked. This can all be acceptable on television, where the interviewer is trying to corner or trip up a politician, and may well lead to fight, flight and avoidance. Indeed, we are used to disputes between politicians and interviewers, leading occasionally to a walk-out by an aggrieved politician. However it is the antithesis of good performance reviewing, which depends on rapport, empathy and establishing common objectives. We can review the main types of questions within that light. Good questioning helps to provoke thinking and generate information whilst maintaining good interpersonal relationships. There are several types of question which, if used appropriately, can be particularly effective:

- **Open questions**
  - cannot be answered by yes or no (and therefore open up discussion);
  - the respondent answers in their own words;
  - are good for eliciting feelings and attitudes as well as facts and for expanding subjects;
  - are usually prefaced by simple interrogatives such as what, how and why.

Examples: *'What were your main achievements last year?'*
'Tell me more about ...?'
'How do you feel about ...?'

- **Closed questions**
  - can be answered by yes or no (and so close down discussion);
  - may be used for relaxing a non-talkative person; however, a talkative person may expand, volunteering information;
  - may also be used for summarising, clarifying or controlling – particularly when faced with vague and unspecific answers to questions.

Examples: *'Did you enjoy the training course?'*
'Are you going to be within budget?'
'So you left BP because of the long hours?'

- **Specific questions**
  - to establish definite information or specific fact;
  - can be used to control the garrulous and clarify information.

Examples: *'What year was it when you joined the squash club?'*
'Who do you deal with in accounts section?'

- **Reflective questions**
  - reflect back, as a rephrased statement, something interesting that somebody has said, usually encouraging the other to expand;
  - can be used to show that you understand an individual's point of view without necessarily showing agreement.

These questions are useful where emotions and strong feelings may be involved, to get more depth of response.
Examples: *'... and they made me feel really welcome'*
'So you feel that the squash club takes an interest in new members'
'... and I think it is a waste of time and money'
'So you wish you had never joined the squash club'

There are certain questions which are unhelpful in a review interview – leading questions, trick questions and marathon questions spring to mind. None of these create rapport between the two parties; they only result in suspicion.

If the aim is to get a more detailed contribution, then the most useful question is the open one. With the right non-verbal communication and listening skills it displays a real interest in what the other person has to say without being too interrogative, biased or dominant. The reflective question is also a helpful form of question during a review or appraisal interview. The interviewer who is genuinely interested in another person's attitudes, feelings, values and beliefs will use mostly these two types of question. For the manager it requires much less thought about what to say and more about what is heard, particularly when the answers to questions generate further interesting supplementary questions.

Listening Listening is an underrated skill, and is often regarded as passive. We often 'filter-listen', trying to pick out key words and phrases. The filter is our own attitudes and biases; in other words, we only hear what we *want* to hear. There are many reasons why people don't listen during performance reviews or development discussions:

- They feel they have something important to say and are determined to say it, whatever else is said.
- They are preoccupied in preparing a counter proposal, defence, qualification or rebuttal to what is being said.
- They are not interested in, nor stimulated by, what is being said to them.
- There are no sanctions involved and no real requirement to act upon what is being said – ie the message is unimportant to them and has a low personal priority for action.
- The message is being filtered and coloured by personal prejudices, by status/pecking order, or because the listener feels threatened by what is being said.
- Previous personal experience of the individual shows he usually has too much to say, has nothing of value to offer or that what he says is too complex, banal or irrelevant.
- The listener may equate listening with inactivity and therefore a waste of time and money – action is preferable to reflection for many people who scarcely regard listening as an activity at all.
- There may be distractions such as physical characteristics, dress, appearance, manner, speech or a noisy and distracting environment.
- There may be a considerable difference in perception and/or comprehension between speaker and listener and, therefore, their respective frames of reference.

People do listen, however, when there are no distractions and where there is an incentive to do so:

- when 'rewards and punishments' are under discussion and they stand to lose or gain;
- when they respect the speaker or they recall that listening has been to their benefit in the past – or alternatively, they are listening to find a flaw in the speaker's argument;
- when the message relates directly to something they are doing and accountable for, and may feel strongly about.

Effective listening is active, rather than passive. It consists of acknowledgement (response) and reflective listening. *Acknowledgment responses* (nods, smiles, mm-hmms, really's!, etc.) encourage the speaker to say more – they show that the listener is engaged by the subject and understands (but not necessarily agrees with) the speaker. *Reflective listening*, ie rephrasing the crucial parts of what someone says to you and returning it to the speaker – is a non-judgemental way of establishing understanding. It has the effect of preventing misunderstandings and showing acceptance of the speaker whilst defusing emotion.

Developing rapport It is important for managers to develop rapport with their staff during review and appraisal interviews. In effect, this involves getting on the same wavelength as the other person. The skills we have already reviewed – listening and questioning – are part of developing rapport. It is important to start and finish the review or appraisal on a positive note, always aiming to reach agreement and find some common ground. The following actions all help to develop rapport:

- Taking an open, non-judgemental stance.
- Matching tone and pitch of voice and, if possible, posture during the interview. For example, if someone is particularly upset or angry, it does not help to develop rapport if the boss is millpond calm and unruffled – it is likely only to aggravate the other person. It is not necessary to become angry yourself, but it would help to inject a pace and movement into your conversation which goes some way to matching their own.
- Minimising differences in grammar and vocabulary, in particular avoiding jargon.
- Concentrating on positives and areas of agreement rather than emphasising negatives.
- When discussing poor performance, focus on performance issues, whilst retaining respect for the individual as a person.
- Asking open questions.

- Listening carefully for the other person's *hidden* agendas, not just the overt content of their message

These skills are critical for the performance review and development review interviews. If effectively carried out, these interviews provide important information for other processes which have a bearing on good performance management.

Career planning

Career planning is the link process between two cycles – the individual performance cycle and the organisational human resource planning process. So far we have seen the performance review processes as an interaction between the line manager and the member of staff. The things they agree between them as relating to work targets and management style are largely within their competence to put into practice.

During the development review the two parties talk about the accretion of skills and knowledge over a time period. They are also likely to discuss the concept of career development in more detail. There are two ways in which individuals progress through organisations; they either develop in the job they are doing or they make step change developments which we normally call promotion. As with the process of continuous improvement, development is normally a combination of those two factors. There is a period of growth through development of competence with the occasional step change when someone is promoted.

The development discussion process tends to take into account the incremental development of skill and knowledge as this is largely within the competence of the line manager and the subordinate. The issue of promotion, however, is more likely to require some form of outside intervention, unless the promotion is within the manager's own area of responsibility. The process of career planning, therefore, also requires connection to a centrally operated system relating to the assessment of potential and other decisions relating to promotion.

The concept of career planning is changing radically. It is no longer possible to construct a detailed plan setting out the main milestones of a career. With the reduction in levels of staff in most organisations, the likelihood of promotion is becoming less and the tendency now is for more people to develop continuously but effectively within their current role. Development, therefore, has become continuous rather than a stop/go process and managers can no longer relax after promotion; promotion normally creates a need for them to extend their skills and knowledge even further.

There are a number of things which, in my opinion, organisations should be looking at with regard to career planning in the demanding environment in which they find themselves.

Young people should be given responsibility as early as possible. Management trainee and management development programmes should emphasise the need for them to take more authority and be held accountable at a much earlier stage. Young managers tend to spend a long time on training programmes before they are finally given something responsible to do. This is a luxury which organisations can no longer afford and they should be giving higher levels of responsibility sooner, whilst ensuring that there is appropriate support and guidance for a more demanding role.

Instead of vertical promotion ladders we should be thinking more of scrambling nets. Rosabeth Moss Kanter in her book *When Giants Learn to Dance* talks about the scrambling net career advancement style, with much more emphasis on horizontal, rather than vertical, fast tracking. This has the effect of moving people around the organisation and having a much broader, rather than a narrow, functional business perspective. In the old style pyramidal promotion, people got to very high levels within their own function before becoming a 'general manager'. In many organisations this had led to narrow functional views taking precedence over the business as a whole. The combination of early responsibility with some movement across the business creates a much broader understanding of the total business.

The process of career planning needs to be extended to cover a range of issues rather than just pure career management. Career planning is also about renewal and redirection and it is important to be aware that, in the future, managers will need to redirect and replenish their skills and knowledge to meet their organisation's needs on a much more regular basis than has taken place so far. This involves the organisation predicting the level of skills it requires from its staff on a regular basis. The process of career planning is the link between the organisation's human resource plans and individual expectations.

Assessment of potential

Assessment of potential cannot be done by a single manager assessing the potential of his team. It is a fallacious use of the performance appraisal system to encourage managers to do this. It is almost inevitable that most of us see our subordinates as only having potential up to our own level and rarely beyond! Within a development review it is reasonable for a manager to comment on development needs and training needs; it may also be reasonable to make a judgement about the potential of an individual to do their manager's own job. However, when a boss is asked to look more broadly across the whole organisation and to make predictions about performance at much higher levels, or in other functions, or even in other countries, then that judgement becomes extremely fallible and to give it more than a low weighting in the overall view of potential assessment is very dangerous. It is, therefore, very important to separate the assessment of potential from the normal appraisal process. There is no reason why the line manager should not be asked for a view of potential, but it should be only a speculative and low-priority view.

In order for potential to be assessed effectively, there is a need for some objective measures across the organisation or at least across certain parts of it. That global view is very important and needs to be underpinned by a common system, using common measurements. It is not a part of the objectives of this book to go into detail about how the assessment of potential should be carried out, but there are a number of objective measures which should be carefully investigated by an organisation in order to ensure that the assessment is carried out in the most effective way. These include:

- psychological tests which can be very helpful if they are valid;
- structured individual or panel interviews, which again can be very helpful if they are based on valid criteria;
- assessment centres which normally combine in-tray and other individual processes with group discussion, group tasks and interviews. These need to be very well designed against clear and objective criteria. To be effective and credible, they must be seen as providing a level playing field for all candidates.

It is important for the organisation to consider how it is going to assess potential. A well established system of assessment centres may work well for some organisations, but may be seen as ineffective in others. If a system of assessment is well designed and credible, then it also needs to be connected to training and development needs analysis, so that people get the benefit of the training they require before they are assessed. The assessment process can then validate the training and development processes within the organisation. Whatever method is used should be based on a clear understanding of the broad competencies required to achieve the company's mission for the future.

There are a couple of caveats for organisations who have not yet operated an assessment of potential programme. One of them is to take potential one step at a time. I have seen assessment of potential exercises carried out in large complex organisations, particularly clearing banks, where people were given a grading of likely ultimate potential which was many levels above their current level in the organisation – this is a dangerous exercise because it creates very high expectations in the individual which may not always be fulfilled. It is also unlikely to be accurate because by the time they reach that level several years later the jobs may have changed. Director and senior manager roles in a large organisation may have particular competency requirements now, but to assess a young manager on the basis of those is likely to produce a series of clones of the current board when it is likely that the jobs will themselves change significantly within that period of time.

Succession planning

Succession planning relates very closely to the assessment of potential and uses the information generated by that process to put names to jobs for the future. Succession planning is an important strategic process and it needs to be gone through regularly in order to reassure the organisation that it has people capable of taking on more senior roles; it also acts as a prompt to individual line managers to review their own succession plans. It is interesting to note that many large decentralised organisations have still kept the succession planning process as one of the core strategic processes in the business to be retained at the centre.

One of the limitations of some traditional methods of succession planning is that it is often used only for senior jobs and beyond, creating 'crown princes' who have the most superbly planned career in contrast to the people who do the work in the organisation, and who are very lucky if they receive any career guidance or career development at all. We should be encouraging succession planning in all units within an organisation. This would enable every manager to consider their unit's structure, present and future, and the people who they would put into those jobs within that structure. This has the effect of making 'people planning' a key strategic process throughout the organisation.

Whilst there must always be a process of identifying a top cadre of potential senior executives capable of operating and resourcing the company's requirements globally, they should not be the only people who have effective career planning.

The technology of succession planning should be very simple and Figure 9 shows a very basic succession plan that I have used in several organisations. It needs to point out crisis succession, the classic dilemma of a key executive running under a bus, but also short-term and long-term succession. A description of development needs is critical (in other words those things that need to be done to ensure that the succession plan is

Job/ incumbent	Crisis succession	Succession within 2 yrs	Succession 2-5 yrs	Development needs	Career path for current incumbent

Figure 9 *Succession plan*

actually fulfilled), as is identifying the career path for the current job incumbent. Input from succession planning should be fed back into the performance management process, normally at development review level, or alternatively in a more formal exercise of communicating the succession plan, so that individuals develop a better understanding of where their career aspirations match the corporate ideas on succession.

It is very disappointing to set out a detailed succession planning process, only to find that many of the individuals within that process do not want to take up the career path which is set out for them. Succession planning is not a once and for all process; it is iterative and the succession plan needs to be a dynamic document – a 'snapshot' of a complex process.

One of the great criticisms of succession plans is that they are never actually fulfilled and this is because they become an annual or once every two year event. Succession plans need to be reviewed regularly by a relatively small group of people and communicated to the management team. They should not just be carried out at a senior level and devolved down; they should be carried out at the appropriate level in the organisation to put the plan into operation but with sufficient distance to be detached and objective.

A number of issues relating to performance management can result from the succession planning process; one is the increasing phenomenon of the 'plateaued manager'. As levels are reduced within organisations and promotion becomes less regular, there is clearly going to be an increase in people within the organisation who have reached what is rather unkindly called their terminal grade. It is important to recognise, however, that there are two ways of developing in the job – incremental development of competence and step change promotion. The former is becoming much more important than the latter, so that even though a person may have reached a level (in job grade terms) from which they will not progress, nevertheless in the next few years they are bound to need to develop new skills and new competences in their current job.

The plateaued manager syndrome can be overcome by imaginative career planning, by effective performance management and also by good reward management so that the individual who is continuing to contribute in terms of increased output and increased personal development will still benefit from the company's reward system. Without this approach the plateaued manager will become an increasing problem.

Manpower planning

Effective succession planning needs to be supported and should be one component of a good manpower planning system. Manpower planning needs to be seen in its most broad guise as human resource planning and needs to be carried out effectively. Good human resource planning needs to include both *hard issues* (such as organisation design, quantative planning techniques, productivity measures), and *soft issues* (such as recruitment methods, development and training and career path analysis).

The objective of manpower planning should, quite simply, be to identify the quantity and quality of people required for the future. This is, of course, an appalling simplification which would cause tremors of rage in any self-respecting manpower planning specialist. However, the manpower planning function has expanded in recent years from its statistical heartland to take a wider view of the organisation and add on several qualitative processes to the traditional quantitative methods. If we are going to measure performance effectively then we have to measure our utilisation of people effectively and, without drowning in a sea of turnover statistics, keep that clearly under review. The monitoring of key statistics such as labour turnover, duration of individuals in job, length of service and so on are important and need to be made available as a key part of the organisation's business planning.

Competence/competency

An important underpinning for all systems relating to personal development is the clarification of competence required to do the job and broader competency which is more useful in relation to assessment of potential. The two factors – *operational competence* and *personal competency* – need to be understood if personal development within the organisation is going to be fully effective.

A clear understanding of operational competences for each job is an effective measure of personal competence in relation to the job. Simply take each critical success factor and identify the skills and knowledge (operational competences) required to carry them out. The next stage is to set down the performance required in each area of competence (see Figure 10).

Equally, a clear understanding of the broader, 'generic' competencies is critical in order to assess potential and develop the individual beyond the core competences of the job. This generic set of competencies is derived in a very different way from the operation competences which are, in effect, brought about by job analysis. The broader competencies are based more on predictions of what is likely to result in success for the organisation. The aim is to cluster into dimensions the behaviour which differentiates

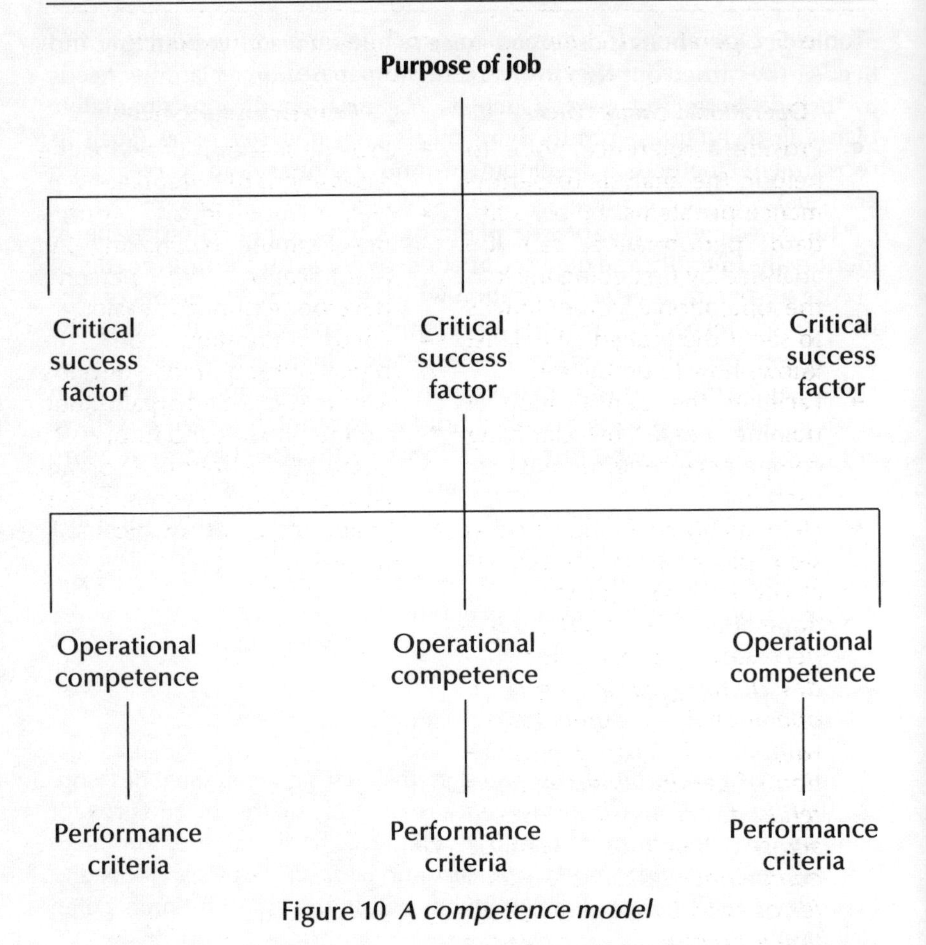

Figure 10 *A competence model*

the high performer, then try to analyse it to enable it to be demonstrated and measured. As Charles Woodruffe comments in his *Personnel Management* article 'Competent by any other name' (September 1991), there is a need to ensure that these competencies are reviewed regularly in order to reflect changes in the organisation's requirements.

The combination of competence and competency is the core to the organisation's performance and capability review processes.

Table 5 *Operational competences and generic competencies: how they affect review processes*

Operational competences	**Generic competencies**
• Provide a reference point to help in the analysis of performance problems. Below standard performance can be analysed by first going back to the operational competences to see if the individual at least knows how to do the job. • Facilitate the identification of training needs by clarifying competence requirements for each job. • Help manpower and succession planning processes by clarifying what needs to be done at each level. (*There is a necessary caveat here – describing jobs in terms of operational competences without a balancing description of generic competencies tends to restrict movement across functions. Generic competencies facilitate transfer of skills by relating operational competences to wider features.*)	• Provide a sound basis for the assessment of potential. • Help individual career development by making the identification of personal development needs easier. • Focus attention on the behaviour required to develop a more successful organisation for the present and future. • Unite all functions of an organisation behind a common language and set of desirable behaviours.

It is important to search for a way of bringing these two key issues together in one common process. A model which works effectively is one which sets out a job as shown in Figure 11.

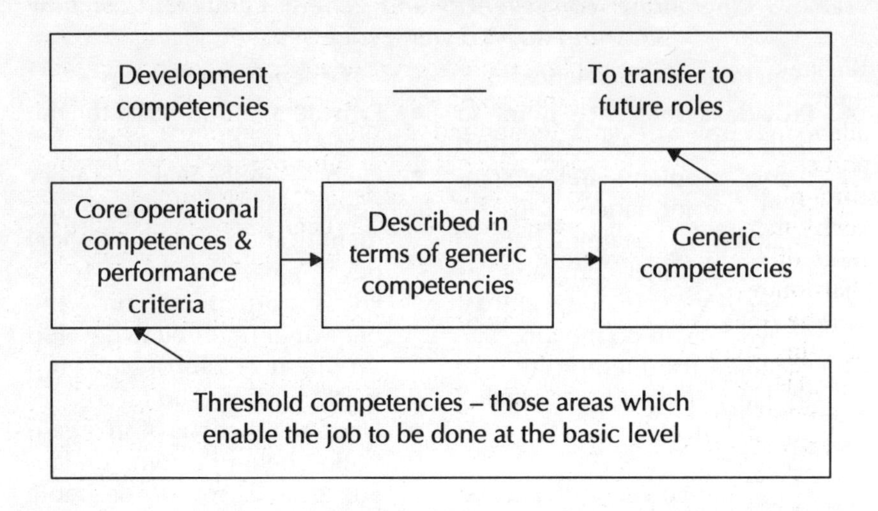

Figure 11 *An effective combination of operational competences and generic competencies*

Boxes overlap each other, so that continuous development from job to job can be as seamless as possible, thus reducing the 'promotion shock effect'.

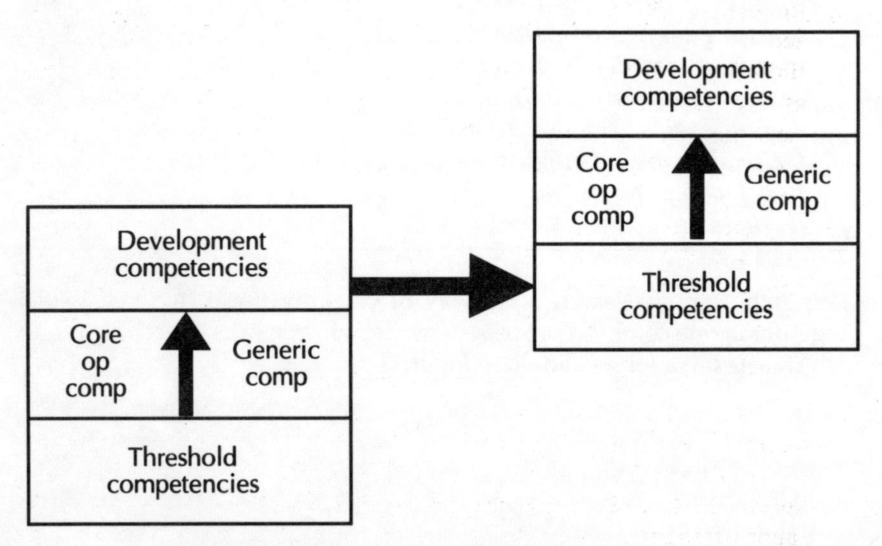

Figure 12 *Linking jobs in a development process*

SUMMARY

We have seen that the process of performance appraisal needs to be split into a number of quite separate functions. This will not, if done correctly, add to the burden of management, but will require a disciplined approach and clear objectives for each performance appraisal process that is gone through. Each of them are iterative insofar as they take information from each other in order to create a coherent set of processes which ensure not only that today's performance is being measured and managed, but that tomorrow's performance is being considered and that the people who are going to deliver that performance are being prepared at an early stage.

Some personnel specialists would see this not as performance management, but as career development, but in my view the two are inseparable and we need to be improving constantly the performance, as well as the skill, knowledge and attitude of individuals. The organisation needs to look ahead because, unlike information technology, our human resources cannot suddenly switch to do something else. We need to equip people with the skills, knowledge and attitudes for the new tasks which face them in the future – *today* – as part of a disciplined performance management process.

AGENDA FOR CHANGE I – carrying out an effective performance review meeting

The objective of the performance review meeting is, quite simply, to examine and review in some detail both sides of the performance contract. It leads on to three possible sets of actions for each area – maintaining current levels of performance; increasing performance requirements when they are being met and reviewing support requirements where elements of the contract are not being met. Any review or appraisal-type interview should take into account the following:

- The first part of the interview needs to focus on building rapport between manager and subordinate. The contract has two parties, both of whom have rights and obligations. If either of the parties approach the meeting as a negotiation, or worse a disciplinary or grievance meeting, then the ethos of the performance contract will be lost and the meeting will become just another unpleasant discussion to be got through as soon as possible, instead of one which engenders a closer working relationship and acts as a springboard to continuous improvement of the business and continuous development of the individual.

- A good way of developing rapport is to base the structure of the meeting on the consensus-conflict-consensus model which applies to all effective meetings. The rationale of this model is that in any meeting or interview it helps to develop rapport if the agenda is drafted to take first those issues in which both parties are likely to agree so that they can move on to areas of potential disagreement in a more positive state of mind. The meeting should end in consensus so that both parties go away with the memory of a productive meeting fresh in their mind and a high level of commitment to the outcomes from the meeting, with, consequently, much more likelihood of putting them into operation. They will also come to the next meeting with enthusiasm and not trepidation.
- The style of the interview should relate to the development level of the individual. We reviewed earlier the situational leadership model; Figure 13 (based on the situational leadership model of Hersey and Blanchard) should help to clarify how appraisal skills relate to the needs of the individual.

Taking these issues into account, the process follows three stages.

Stage One – Examine the whole job

- How is the job working out? What things have gone well during the period under review? Why have they gone well? What trends are working in our favour and need to be analysed to see if we can get better results?
- What things have not gone well during the period under review? What may have been the cause of this? Are there any obvious barriers to progress in this area?

The positive question is asked first here to gain consensus. It is also used to probe where the individual feels that things are going well – this gives the manager a clue to which areas of the job to start discussing first – the ones in which there is likely to be a good positive outcome.

Stage Two – Examine each critical success factor

- Have the output objectives been met? If so, can they be increased? If not, why not? What can be done to bring them back on track?
- Have the capability objectives been met? Is there scope for greater capability in this area? If the output objectives can be increased, what are the implications for our capability in terms of budget, people, equipment, assets or time?

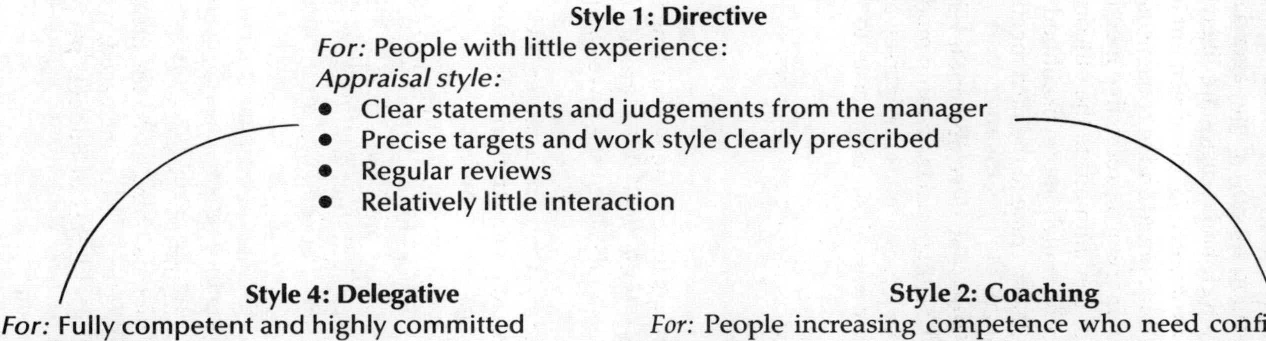

Figure 13 *Interview styles*

If the objectives have been met, then the discussion moves towards reviewing objectives and moving them up a notch for the next review; if they have not been met the discussion moves towards identifying the performance gap and agreeing an action plan to remove it. Both of these issues are dealt with in more depth during the next two chapters.

Stage Three – Redraft the performance contract

The final phase of the review is to go through the performance contract and redraft it to take into account the last period's performance. This process may include some or all of the following:

- Increasing output and capability objectives;
- Reviewing resources available;
- Identifying training needs;
- Changing the management style.

AGENDA FOR CHANGE II – carrying out an effective development review

The performance review and the development review comprise a general stocktaking in relation to the growth of competence, career direction and training and development needs. The two meetings are quite different in approach and style; the performance review is boss-led and analytical; the development review should be subordinate-led and open-ended. The two processes are entirely complementary and the end result will normally be a complete picture of current performance and future direction.

The development review necessitates a change of emphasis for the manager – from boss to coach. In the performance review, the role is one of clarifying, directing and organising; during the development review, the key activities for the manager are advising, supporting and providing a more strategic view of the company's future direction.

The discussion has several important pre-conditions to ensure success. The first is adequate preparation by both parties. They need to come to the discussion with the following information:

- **Manager**
  - A clear view of the competences required to do the current job
  - A view of the organisation's strategic direction and the manpower needs for the future
- **Subordinate**
  - A clear analysis of personal strengths and weaknesses
  - A clear view of their own aspirations and the skills they want to build on for the future.
- **Both**
  - A clear and unambiguous view of the individual's performance against contract over the last year
  - An open mind

The discussion should be between two people who genuinely want to get the most out of an individual – not in a Machiavellian sense but because they both benefit from, and contribute to, maximising the potential of that individual. The meeting *should* be run by the subordinate – it is their job satisfaction and future job development which is at stake. However, it may be more appropriate for it to be led by the manager, depending on the experience and confidence of the individual. An inexperienced and under-confident person leading a discussion only to be 'rescued' by their manager part-way through is counter-productive. The agenda should cover the following:

1. A personal 'SWOT' analysis covering points 2 to 4 below.
2. Ways to use personal strengths in order to maximise future performance.
3. Ways to eradicate relevant limitations to current job performance and future development.
4. A review of the future needs for competence in the job and how the individual's current portfolio of skills meets those needs.
5. The development of an action plan to ensure that these issues are covered and an agreement on how this plan should be reviewed. One option is to build this into the performance contract process – possibly as a critical success factor for self-development.

The development review may well be an annual event – it is a less formal, 'stocktaking' process. It could be attached to a performance review meeting, although it is important to ensure that the two meetings are run separately with quite clearly differentiated objectives, otherwise they become like the old performance appraisal – a mish-mash of discussion covering performance, competence and development without really clarifying which concept is being considered at any time.

9

People who Meet their Contract

Setting the performance contract and reviewing it are obviously two critical parts of the performance cycle; they are worthless, however, unless something is done to *manage* the results of the process. It would be as if the budgeting process stopped once the budget had been agreed and no-one took any action to manage it for the remainder of the year.

The performance contract and performance review mechanisms are part of a cyclical process that involves constant adjustment as circumstances and performance change. There are a number of possible outcomes which arise from the performance review process:

- The individual meets the whole range of performance requirements within the contract.
- The individual fails to meet the whole range of performance requirements within the contract.
- The individual exceeds at least some of the performance requirements within the contract.
- The individual meets some requirements and fails to meet some others.

Within this range of outcomes, there are two categories which demand management action. The manager needs to follow two loops:

1. For those aspects of the contract which have not been met, the manager should go into problem-solving mode to identify the cause of the discrepancy and agree a solution with the individual and an action plan to ensure that these gaps are resolved.
2. For those aspects of the contract which have been met or exceeded, the manager should immediately set a new, higher target to ensure that the momentum is not lost.

Case study

A division of a food manufacturing organisation had several factories, producing a range of fresh and frozen meat products. Two factories were particularly notable in their results:

Factory A was an old abattoir using equipment which had been completely written down and with an experienced non-union workforce. It was producing fresh meat products for airline catering, small butchers and for several multiple retailers. The meat was delivered in primal cuts, so there was very little extra processing to be done in the factory (apart from the airline business where the meat was delivered butchered for the catering process). The factory was producing well, having found some reliable suppliers who had very little bargaining power. The factory had a return on capital of around 35 per cent, largely due to the absence of capital investment and the 'cash cow' nature of its business. Production efficiencies were moderate with a reasonable net margin on its products.

Factory B was a new meat processing plant with expensive equipment and an inexperienced workforce. It was producing a range of prepared foods – some ethnic, some basic meals – for multiple food retailers which necessitated high product development costs. The products were starting to appeal to the microwave cooker market which had only relatively recently been established and so there was a lot of risk in the development areas. The factory had high efficiency ratios and was beginning to attract good gross margin figures but the return on capital was around 18 to 19%, below the organisation's 20% target for each of its strategic business units.

At the next round of performance review meetings, the group managing director complimented the general manager of Factory A for exceeding the return on capital target. He instituted a detailed review of Factory B to try to identify how to improve its business and later set up a series of cost cutting measures to bring the business into line.

At the time, I was the group personnel manager. I argued strongly that whilst we should review Factory B to see how we could improve the business, we should also review Factory A and set new targets for that business. My view was based on the fact that it was a business with relatively few costs; it was not as efficient as it could be and it was in a mature market. Every trend was working for it and I felt that it was more sensible to put our management resources into getting more output from Factory A than trying to squeeze even more out of the already highly efficient Factory B, although a review of Factory B's business would also have been helpful.

This case study, I believe, demonstrates two important issues relating to performance management. One is the folly of only applying across-the-board targets which may be too demanding for some and too easy for others; the second is the importance of re-targeting people who appear to be reaching their performance requirements with ease.

We should certainly help to review the work of our performers who are below requirements; we should also take the opportunity to set more challenging goals for the high achievers and the people who are just meeting their goals. Everyone needs something to aim for and to create an appropriate challenge it should be just a little way over their head so that they need to develop new skills or challenge their own inner reserves to achieve success.

There are two things that we can do when people meet or exceed their contract; either put them onto the track of continuous improvement, or delegate more of our work to them.

CONTINUOUS IMPROVEMENT

The management of performance can only thrive and be effective when there is all-consuming commitment to continuous improvement across the whole range of business objectives. There is a need to achieve continuous improvement in costs, sales, quality and processes whilst encouraging development in structures, people, systems and technology. The two concepts fit neatly into the input/output model – aiming for continuous improvement in the services and products we provide and continuous development of our capability to achieve those service levels.

There are four actions which can be carried out in relation to our business objectives:

- Innovation
- Improvement
- Maintenance
- Removal

Innovation

Innovation is the form of development which creates major step changes in products, processes and services. The effect of innovation is normally dramatic and involves large quantities of capital investment. It is the invention of new technology or a significant transformation in a company's operation, eg a major reorganisation.

Improvement

Improvement involves the incremental improvement of current products, services, systems and procedures. It is a relatively undramatic form of change which consists of two features – the change is gradual and it is constant. To enlarge upon its dictionary definition, improvement is a frame of mind linked to maintaining and improving standards. The Japanese word for continuous improvement, *Kaizen*, has become one of the main building blocks in Japanese industry and society. To the Japanese, Kaizen means on-going improvement in all parts of life and at work.

Maintenance

Maintenance refers to activities that are directed to maintaining current technological, managerial and operating standards within organisations and to keeping their products and services at their current rate of output and quality.

Removal

Removal is the cessation of a particular activity. It underpins the other three factors because, if things are to be improved and developed effectively some redundant activities need to be stopped to prevent them from eating up vital resources and energy.

When conducting a review of our operations we need to assess which functions we should maintain, which functions we need to improve and which new services or products we need to develop. The fourth category – things that we need to drop – is also a critical decision for management. Too often we dissipate our energy on 'futile and hopeless labour' (remember Sisyphus?) when that energy would be more effectively harnessed in improving another area of our operation or developing something new.

Continuous improvement is critical to the work of every organisation if we are to do more than just maintain our levels of service. If all our operational energies were focused on maintenance, we would, in effect, be regressing in relation to those of our competitors who were focusing on greater improvement and development.

The implications of continuous improvement for performance management are very significant. I began the book by referring to the emancipation of Sisyphus. The concept of continuous improvement is critical to the emancipation of people within the organisation. It is no longer sufficient just to turn up and do a reasonably good job to an agreed standard.

Organisations will cease to be effective unless people come into work determined to improve, albeit in small incremental steps, the quality of the work they do in every area of their operation. If everyone increased their output by only 1 per cent each month, think of the impact on the organisation, particularly if they reduced their costs by 1 per cent over the same period.

The implications of continuous improvement for performance management are as follows:

- Any set of objectives – organisational, divisional, unit, team or individual should include proposals to maintain, improve, develop or drop services which are currently provided.
- Objectives should always be stretching, but not too stretching; they should allow for an overall improvement in service levels and be constantly reviewed. The achievement of a set of standards and targets should be the signal for a review of those targets and further small increases made.
- People who are currently providing excellent service should be reviewing their capability objectives to ensure that they are equipped to continue to provide excellent service well into the future.
- People also need continuous improvement and development. The continuous development of people needs to work hand in hand with the continuous improvement of product and services. Continuous development is not necessarily achieved by a stream of training courses, but is achieved by setting stretching objectives and providing the necessary management support and direction.

Continuous improvement is based on the concept of making many small improvements across the whole range of operations. It is improving 100 things by 1 per cent, rather than improving one thing by 100 per cent. It relies on the commitment of the whole organisation rather than on a small elite of 'rather creative people in Head Office'. A blend of maintenance, improvement and development should give a performance profile as set out in Figure 14.

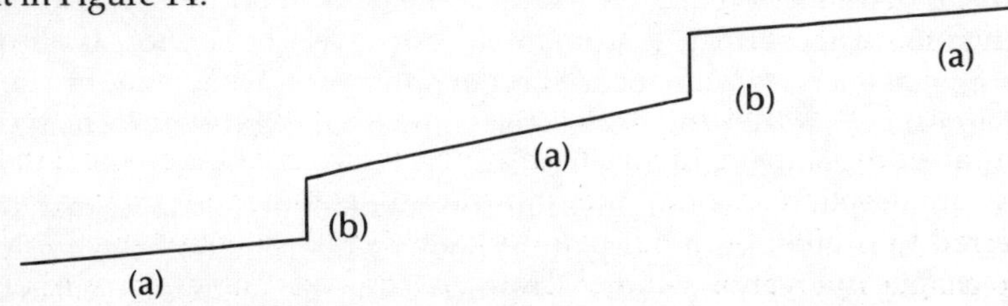

Figure 14 *Performance profile – improvement*

With (a) as a period of improvement and (b) as a new 'quantum leap' development, this contrasts with the innovation/deterioration cycle familiar in many organisations and shown in Figure 15, where (d)

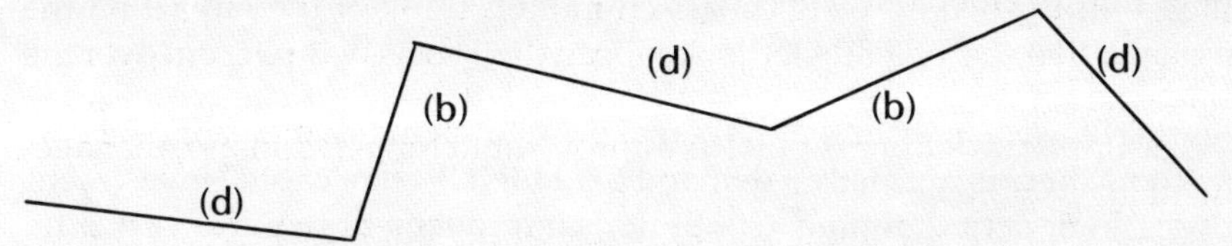

Figure 15 *Performance profile – deterioration*

is the period of deterioration which often follows on from innovation after a period of poor performance management.

Continuous improvement is probably more important than innovation in the long term to most organisations. A combination of continuous improvement, innovation and disciplined maintenance of standards is going to be almost unstoppable in relation to the management of performance. An examination of change across a range of industries demonstrates that most changes taking place are the small, undramatic ones and not necessarily the high profile, dramatic quantum leaps forward. There is no question that organisations need people to be working on those changes which transform a business or an industry, but not at the expense of incremental improvement in product services and procedures. Continuous improvement is, therefore, the secret weapon in the management of performance both organisationally and individually. Why is that?

Immediate impact Everyone within an organisation can make an immediate improvement, however small, to one aspect of their work or operation. Innovation often takes several years to work through and needs to be piloted and tested in detail. As any manager who has taken over a new operation knows, it is easy to find some small successes which can boost morale. The development of a run of small successes can have a tremendous effect on the morale of an organisation or team and the individuals within it.

The concept of continuous improvement which helps to overcome the natural entropy, the tendency to disorder, which has become part of the way organisations work. The innovation/deterioration cycle already referred to is often born out of an organisational strategy which makes step change innovation without the supporting disciplines of continuous improvement and maintenance to ensure that standards in the other part of the operation are maintained. One of Parkinson's laws was that once an organisation has reached its peak, its begins to decline. Innovation, whilst important, is a one-off event whose effects are gradually eroded by intense competition and deteriorating standards. The concept of continuous improvement is an on-going effort with cumulative efforts marking a steady rise as years go by.

Relatively small investment To make huge changes in technology or systems there is normally a demand for a high level of capital investment over a long period of time. Continuous improvement requires very little financial investment although it can require significant investment in terms of personal commitment and discipline from the whole team, and this can take time to generate. Continuous improvement normally involves improving the use of the 'soft' factors in the organisation – people, relationships etc. Another important advantage of continuous improvement in relation to performance management is that a manager within an organisation doesn't need to ask permission to carry it out. It may be that a need arises to talk to top management if continuous improvement programmes involve retraining and rescheduling of staff, however, a manager can make a start on the programme with only himself and his team aware that this is going on. Through making small improvements he can then demonstrate that the programme is worthwhile without having to spend time calculating return on investment figures.

The most successful continuous improvement programmes start to attract attention without the initiators having to publicise them – people start to wonder 'what exactly is going on there?' This is a much more attractive way of raising profile than the 'announcement-itis' which many organisations suffer from – announcing major changes which subsequently fail to live up to their initial expectations.

Continuous improvement applies across the whole organisation thus it can have immediate demonstrable benefits on all parts of the balance sheet. A shortlist of areas for potential improvement projects will demonstrate this:

- Stock availability
- Labour utilisation
- Machine utilisation
- Energy Costs
- Raw material costs
- Processing time
- Stock holding
- Sales calls

and so on. By supporting all parts of the organisation, continuous improvement need not have a distorting effect on the balance sheet whilst still making a significant contribution to the way the organisation operates.

A wide range of staff become involved The process of innovation, particularly in high technology businesses, can involve only a few key staff in 'R and D' type departments. A process of continuous improvement spread throughout the organisation can, indeed *must*, involve everybody within the organisation. Mathematically, this increases the probability of creative ideas coming forward and an organisation of between 50,000 and 60,000 people harnessing the full creative potential of their staff is an awesome prospect.

I am writing this book in the middle of the most significant recession for the British economy over the last ten years. It is also a period when interest rates have been very high and this has had a dampening effect on investment in both labour and capital. Because continuous improvement does not require high levels of investment it, therefore, is a process which is recession proof and, in fact, as an economy goes through a recession, organisations need to look carefully at ways to improve their product and service offer to the customer without adding to their costs. From the Japanese experience, there is no doubt that continuous improvement is a recession proof way of increasing profit.

The concept of continuous improvements fits neatly into the performance management model. It lifts performance management from merely meeting our targets to a constant process of meeting targets, reframing them, meeting them again and reframing in what should become an upward spiral. It avoids what has become known as 'Chinese Horoscope' management – 'This year is the year of the customer' or 'Our year of quality'. Continuous improvement means that *every* year has to be the year of everything – the quiet and undramatic achievement of increasingly stretching objectives. For every critical success factor in which objectives are met, the performance review meeting should produce a reframed performance requirement; challenging enough to stretch, available enough to reach and interesting enough to want to strive for.

DELEGATION

The second option available to the manager is the delegation of his own work. Delegation is a key skill in the management of performance and has relevance both at the organisational level and at the managerial level. The objective of any process of delegation is threefold – the freeing up of time for strategic thinking, the raising of levels of initiative amongst less experienced staff and the greater involvement of people within the organisation in the ways in which they carry out their work. The latter is the area which is most often neglected. If, instead of 20 people doing the creative thinking on process and method, the organisation can enlist 1000 people working on their own objectives in their own way, it is likely to generate far more creative alternatives; a critically important factor during a time of intense competitive pressure.

The essence of delegation is to manage the 'what', 'where' and 'when' whilst leaving the 'how' to the delegate. This allows clear objectives to be set and monitored, whilst allowing the method or process to be, to a greater or lesser extent depending on their experience, at the discretion of the individual who is carrying out the task. The effective delegator sets clear objectives and sketches out the boundaries of the task before allowing the delegate to get on with the job in their own unique way. A further element of delegation is the need to agree the support and direction that the individual will need from their boss.

Organisations delegate tasks and authority to subordinate units. They do so because a small strategic business unit may be closer to a particular market, thus authority is delegated to an appropriate level to get the job done by the person or unit who understands it best. They then set business targets, monitor those targets regularly and concentrate on strategic review of the business rather than operational interference. The most successful organisations in highly devolved businesses are those, like Hanson and GEC, who have kept their hands off their businesses, but their eyes on the key results.

In a similar way, managers delegate tasks and authority to members within their team. This mechanism is the main process through which all managers grow and develop – both the delegator who develops by learning to manage a process rather than operate it and the delegate who grows by taking on work at a higher level of complexity or difficulty.

There is also a process of *lateral delegation* which is an important issue in organisational development. Specialist functions are developing new products, systems and approaches which the mainstream 'generalist' parts of the organisation need to adopt and adapt in order to achieve their constantly increasing levels of service. These new systems often remain with their specialist initiators instead of becoming part of the work of the general managers. The specialist department needs to share its initiatives in a stable and orderly fashion in order to ensure that the new initiatives are implemented effectively. Many organisational disputes arise because of poor lateral delegation – either the specialists dump it onto the implementers and run, or they regard it as part of their organisational territory and retain it for too long.

There are four key issues which relate to delegation:

1. Clarification of what can be delegated and what should not be;
2. The selection of the task and the person;
3. The effective handover; and
4. The level of monitoring.

These are important because if we are to delegate authority as far as possible, it will need to be carried out effectively.

EF Schumacher in his book *Small is Beautiful* put the principle of subsidiary of function as the first principle in deciding how large organisations should be structured. He quoted extensively from a previous Papal Encyclical as follows:

> It is an injustice and at the same time a grave evil and disturbance of right order to assign to a greater and higher association what lesser and subordinate organisations can do.

He expressed the view that subsidiary parts of an organisation would create a closer bond to the organisation as a whole if they felt that their role was clear and they were fulfilling themselves rather than operating as the implementers of someone else's ideas. It is one of the many paradoxes of management that, by releasing day-to-day control, we increase the overall adhesion of the organisation. The Papal Encyclical goes on:

> In observing the principle of subsidiary function the stronger will be the social authority and effectiveness and happier and more prosperous the condition of the state.

Delegation, therefore, is clearly an important strategic process which even has Papal support. Organisations do it, managers do it. If we combine delegation with continuous improvement we have a very effective strategy for improving the business and developing the people. It economises on research and development and training programmes, although it does involve a high level of time and commitment on the part of managers, and needs to be effectively carried out so that the work stays at the subsidiary level and continues to free up senior management to think strategically. We have already identified the issues that delegators have to face; we shall now review them individually.

What can be delegated and what should not be

When a manager examines his job to see what he can delegate, he needs to be sure that it is something he should be delegating. Within our bundle of critical success factors there are things which are so critical to our own effectiveness that we should not, under any circumstances, delegate. In my experience these are:

- **Responsibility for staff development.** We can never wholly delegate away our responsibility for the management and development of the people who work for us. The responsibility for setting performance contracts, reviewing them and providing direction and support must always stay primarily with the line manager. I say primarily, because we may involve other, more experienced subordinates in a peer coaching/mentor-type role with new starters, if we feel that they have an important input into a new starter's development. This is delegating some activity; it cannot be seen as delegating accountability, which should remain with us.
- **Responsibility for setting the strategic direction of the unit.** The manager can, and indeed should, invite participation in the mission building process. However, he must bring together the strategic direction of the unit into one coherent plan. This is one of the key management leadership functions which cannot be delegated to others.
- **Administrative trivia.** Delegating the boring parts of certain jobs aggregated into a dull package of administrative trivia is also a mistake. It may fulfil a need to clear away some administrative debris but it will not fulfil the other objective of developing people to take on more interesting work; in fact it will make them more resistant to the whole notion of delegation. If the work is so trivial, it may be better to dump it completely.

Otherwise a manager can delegate whatever parts of their job will provide development opportunities for one of their team, providing that it is a whole chunk of a job and not an unconnected group of administrative tasks. The critical decisions are the marrying of an appropriate task to the right person.

Selection of the task and the person

It is not always possible to delegate the work that we most want to dispense with. I have spent most of my career trying to delegate the responsibility for the setting up and monitoring of budgets and have not always found a suitable person to receive them. When I have, however, they have been delegated with quite startling rapidity.

The decision to delegate work must be based on a sensible development plan for a subordinate, a part of which is the taking on of a particular element of their manager's work. The first issue has to be – when is someone ready to accept delegated work? It is important to recognise, at this stage, that delegation is a process of handing work from a manager to their subordinate, ie it is the manager's work which is being delegated. Quite often managers believe that they are delegating when they are merely giving people the authority to do their own work without interference. This only creates the illusion of delegation.

People are ready to accept delegated work when they are fully competent to handle their own work without interference. If they are working well in some areas and not in others, delegation would be premature until the performance contract is being met across the full range of critical success factors. Delegation should, however, be the next stage of an individual's development. The objective, either output or capability, may be the management of a function or project of which the subordinate already operates a significant chunk but at a lower level. It may be the co-ordination of other projects within the department. It may be to take responsibility for introducing a new system or organisational change. Whatever it is, it needs to be quite clearly focused on a development need for the individual and so the manager should ask:

- What are they good at? How can I capitalise on this? (It is better to delegate a project with a high likelihood of success – it helps achieve everyone's objectives).
- What will they be doing in the future? Can I help them develop new skills to help them to succeed in this?

The likelihood is that the right thing to delegate will fall into these two categories – something they currently do well which the manager can enhance; and something they will need to do well in the future which the manager can introduce.

The handover

The critical area in delegation is the handover. Delegation is quite a different concept from abdication. Delegation takes place gradually over a period of time; abdication takes place overnight. Students of history will be aware of the two models of colonial disentanglement: the British, who were accused by their detractors of handing over power too slowly to their colonies, and the Belgians, who were accused of handing over power too quickly, particularly in The Congo.

These are two extremes for organisations to avoid. If power is handed over too slowly the delegate becomes frustrated and expends valuable energy in trying to extract increasing levels of authority from the manager. Conversely, if the decision to devolve authority is followed up almost immediately by a massive dumping operation, in which the manager hands over authority too rapidly, the delegate expends a great deal of energy in floundering about and trying to identify what they ought to be doing and how.

The handover in any delegation situation – either organisational or individual – should be undertaken slowly, following a process of incremental development. This means setting out initially what needs to be done and how it should be carried out. Once this has been achieved, the principal can start to hand over authority and give less direction. The delegate still needs to be well-supported, however, and this process is continued over a period of time until the manager, and more importantly, the delegate feels confident enough to accept full responsibility for the particular task. Even at this stage there should be no abdication of responsibility on the part of the manager and a regular review should be set up to ensure that high levels of performance are being sustained.

Whilst it is very important to ensure that both parties to the performance contract understand what is expected of them, it is equally important that other people in the organisation understand what has happened in the delegation process. Part of the process of delegation is to free up time for the manager. This will not be achieved if people still keep coming to them with issues which have been devolved by the manager to another person. It is important, therefore, to make quite clear that this is a matter of deliberate managerial strategy and that the people who need to know – other staff in the organisation or team, customers and so on – should be clearly informed and an appropriate method of operation structure clarified.

Essentially, the newly delegated work becomes an additional clause to the performance contract, although it should be seen initially as an addendum rather than as part of the main body of the contract. Only when it has been effectively handed over and both parties are entirely happy can it then be embodied into the main contract. Delegation always contains some element of risk and it would be wrong if someone felt penalised in the company's performance related pay scheme by taking on some work which distorted the achievement of their own performance contract.

Monitoring

A final issue is the question of monitoring performance. This is part of the issue of handover and effective monitoring should take place regularly. Even though work has been devolved to a subordinate, nevertheless it remains the manager's responsibility to ensure that it is carried out effectively. This can now be done very easily by the use of effective information systems, and, as we have seen, part of the performance contract is to agree the measures which will ensure that this is being done satisfactorily.

There are two main monitoring styles which need to be avoided – at one extreme, giving someone a job to do then going back constantly to see how they are doing; at the other extreme, handing it over and dashing off to leave them with it for ever. Managers should remember that they can delegate authority and accountability but that the job remains part of their performance contract and so they can't entirely wipe it from their memory. It is in the manager's own interest to ensure that the job is being carried out effectively. Monitoring must be done as part of the performance cycle, not on the basis of sporadic harassment.

Two other issues relating to delegation are 'permissions' and 'monkeys'.

You have to give people permission when you delegate. Permission to do things in their own way. Permission to do things differently than you do them. Permission to bring their own personality to their work. Permission to be left alone to get along with their job. Permission to come and see you when they really need help.

Which brings us onto monkeys. William Oncken and Donald Wass in their famous article 'Managing Management Time – Who's got the Monkey' *Harvard Business Review*, November 1974 says that every subordinate with a problem in their boss's office has a monkey on their back waiting to jump onto their bosses back. Don't take monkeys back – a job, when it has been delegated, should *stay* delegated. Coach them, help them, support them but don't insult them by taking the job back, even if they desperately want you to. If you've delegated effectively and in stages, there should be no stage when it becomes too much to handle.

10

Resolving Performance Problems

The issue of people who have not met some or all of their performance requirements, and the consequences for the performance review is an important one. In a system of cascading performance contracts the consequences of failing to meet requirements are three-fold:

1. The individual fails to meet their performance contract and may, therefore, where contracts are tied to a system of remuneration, incur some financial loss.
2. The manager fails to meet his own performance contract through the failure of one of his team to achieve part of their contract.
3. The whole team fails to meet their performance contracts with other parts of the organisation.

The reasons for not achieving required performance are potentially endless. People are complex entities operating within complex organisations. We have already discussed the ecological nature of performance, that it depends on the relationship between people and the organisation. When we start to deal with performance problems, we have to work hard to discover the possible cause: this may relate to the individual, the organisation, the relationship between the two or the individual's relationship with their manager. The latter is the most difficult for managers to resolve as it involves a close scrutiny of their own effectiveness. Because of the complexity of people and the increasingly disparate nature of organisations, problem resolution has to begin with a careful diagnosis of the reasons for non-achievement of performance requirements. The alert reader will have noticed that I have not used the expression 'poor performance', rather I have either referred to 'non-achievement of' and 'not meeting' performance requirements, or to performance problems. This is deliberate; it is a more practical approach because it encourages people to focus on a tangible problem which needs to be resolved. Poor performance is an expression or term used by people who have not been able to specify the precise nature of the performance problem and so tend to categorise it vaguely: like the doctor who tells you that you are a sick person but can't explain the nature of the illness.

It is also important to bear in mind that I am talking here of *performance* problems, not behavioural, attitudinal or 'personality' problems. There is a danger here of getting bogged down in a philosophical debate about the relationship between performance, behaviour, attitude and personality. The view that underpins this book and this chapter is that good performance management, by identifying, and resolving the performance issues, should enable some other issues to be resolved as well – attitude and behaviour in particular. Managing or trying to change personality is a different issue altogether and one which is largely beyond the remit of organisations or the managers within them. Performance management is about what people *do*, not what they are.

Performance problems need to be resolved like any other problem in a commercial organisation. Diagnosis needs to precede solution; the solution needs to be implemented effectively and reviewed regularly to ensure that it remains the correct solution. Many managers, when faced with performance problems, act like those overworked GPs who prescribe medicine for a patient instead of diagnosing the cause of the illness. The manager wants to find an immediate solution and reaches for some sort of quick remedy – ranging from a training course to formal disciplinary proceedings, depending on their mood and the severity of the problem.

Time spent in careful diagnosis, however, is likely to result in a more effective solution, and therefore resolves the problem with the minimum of ill-will. In fact, there are few greater opportunities to cement a working relationship than working together constructively to resolve a performance problem.

PROBLEM SOLVING – THE VARIOUS STAGES

There are a number of stages which need to be gone through in a problem-solving exercise.

Problem identification

This is a precise description of the gap between the required and actual performance. It relates to the performance contract and the requirements set out there. It is important to be able to state clearly and unequivocally, without blame or malice, where the problem exists. Both parties can then focus on this performance gap to try and identify what has caused it.

Problems are normally associated with change. They can occur when some of the following situations arise:

- a well tried process suddenly goes off track;
- a new system fails to meet performance expectations;
- the environment changes and a system fails to meet the new challenge.

For 'system' and 'process' read 'performance' or 'people'. The essence of all these things is change, even the start-up problem is connected, albeit vaguely, with something not going according to plan. The diagnosis has to focus on what has changed (see Figure 16). A is the agreement on performance, B is the performance requirements and C is the point where performance began to vary from requirements and ended up at D. The performance gap is from B to D.

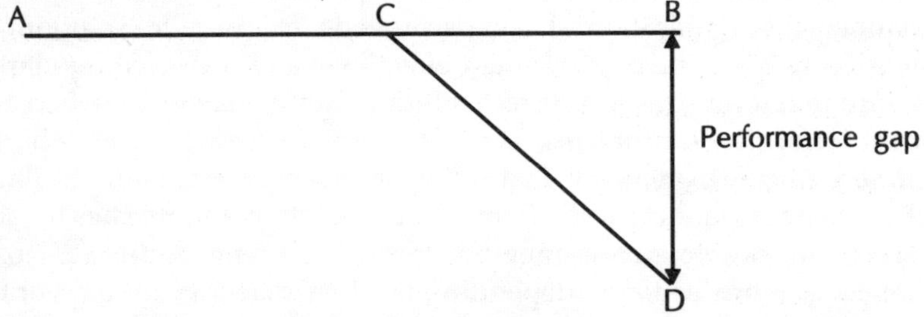

Figure 16 *Diagnosing performance problems*

Problem-solving is most effective the nearer it is to point C, which is an important reason for reviewing performance regularly in order to ensure that off-track performance is picked up early.

Problem specification.

To find out why performance has moved away from plan, we need to compare where performance meets requirements and where it fails to meet requirements. The thinking behind this is that it is highly unlikely that people will fail to meet every element of their performance contract. We should ensure that we understand which objectives are being met and which are not being met: a simple list will do for this. In the unlikely event of them failing to meet the whole performance contract, we should look back to a time when they did meet the whole, or even part of, their contract, to get some hard facts about the person and their performance.

The next part of problem-specification is an analysis of that information. Why do they meet requirements in some areas and not others? Are there any trends which can be discerned? Are there new skills, changes in management, reductions in resources, different people to deal with, a change in customer base, a recent promotion or the introduction of some new members of staff or a reallocation of duties? The list is probably endless and needs to be reconciled by good analysis – comparing the factors rigorously with the information available in order to avoid hasty acceptance of some 'obvious' solution which pops up at an early stage in the process, to avoid more thorough analysis.

This is a joint process – both parties should pool their information, particularly if the manager is very new and has very little historical perspective of the problems of past performance. There is little point in both parties agonising over the situation in their respective offices – they need to get together to sort out what is, after all, a joint problem.

Problem diagnosis

The process of identifying causes from the analysis of symptoms. It can only operate when there is clear agreement on the nature of the problem and its precise specification.

Solution identification

This is based closely on the accurate diagnosis of cause. Because this and problem diagnosis operate closely together, we will review some of the likely causes of performance problems, particularly as they relate to the putting together of the performance contract. There are also a range of issues which relate to some of the organisational barriers which stand in the way of individual performance.

CAUSES OF PERFORMANCE PROBLEMS

Gaps

There are various gaps which may appear to take up the major part of the performance gap:

- Competence gap – the gap between performance requirements and the individual's capacity to achieve them.
- Capability gap – the gap between output objectives and the appropriate capability objectives.
- Appraisal gap – the absence of clear and measurable feedback on performance.

- Resource gap – the absence of sufficient resources to carry out the performance contract.
- Authority gap – the individual doesn't have the necessary authority to carry out the performance contract.
- Motivation gap – when the individual isn't committed to achieving the performance requirements.
- Direction gap – when the individual isn't clear about the precise nature of what is expected of them.
- Reward gap – when the individual doesn't feel rewarded or recognised for their work.

Competence Gap the competence gap occurs when an individual lacks either a key skill or the essential knowledge which would enable them to do their job. The key question which will identify this element is 'Have they *ever* been able to do the job or a particular part of it?' If they have performed effectively in that part of the job in the past, then they cannot be said to lack competence and the cause has to lie elsewhere. One of the great illusions in management problem-solving is that of competent people suddenly becoming incompetent. There is a ratchet effect in relation to competence which prevents us from sliding back down the competence scale – swimming and riding a bicycle are two examples. Our skills in both may become a little rusty over the years but our fundamental ability to do them – after a fashion – does not change. There are two further issues in relation to competence that we need to examine:

1. Skills, if under-used, can become stale and we may need to arrange for someone with a record of skilled achievement but with little recent operational experience to practice their skills before they are needed. After a long period of absence from acting as a classroom trainer, I had to return to lead some senior management programmes in a company for which I was personnel manager. The feeling I had reminded me of the first innings of the cricket season – surviving but not timing the ball quite as well as I should! A little practice in the nets would have been helpful; a little practice in rusty skills at work helps bring performance back on track.
2. Our level of competence may be overtaken by events and our business environment may suddenly make demands on us beyond the level that we can handle competently. When this happens, we have not suddenly become incompetent; we simply need to raise our skills and knowledge up to the new level now required of us.

The solution to a competence gap needs careful analysis. The easy solution is a training course, but the range of possible solutions can extend from reading books and attending conferences to in-depth individual coaching. It is important to specify very clearly the things that the individual needs to know or do to meet their performance requirements and to obtain professional support on finding a solution that fills the gap accurately, taking into account the learning style of the individual.

Capability Gap this gap is slightly different from the competence gap insofar as it relates to the gap between the set of output objectives and the corresponding capability (input) objectives. In simple terms, it means that the individual is trying to squeeze too much output from their unit or department without setting up an effective infrastructure. It is the managerial equivalent of running a car without proper servicing or a country without an effective transport system. It doesn't relate to the individual's own personal competence, although it may relate to a failure to train or develop that person to meet their performance requirements.

The solution is to go back over the output objectives and ensure that the right level of capability in terms of systems, structures, material and manpower is available to support the service requirements and that work has been done to improve capability, develop new capabilities and divert resources from redundant projects to ensure that they are focused on the key service objectives.

Appraisal gap the appraisal gap relates to the absence of clear and unambiguous feedback on performance requirements. The individual just does not know how they are doing. This situation can be prevented by disciplined adherence to the performance cycle. However, even within the boundaries of the cycle a number of appraisal gaps can appear:

- The absence of timely and accurate information generated by the organisation's information systems (a school of which I am a governor receives budget information months after the costs have gone through, with little opportunity to manage the variances by the year end).
- Performance reviews which are spaced too far apart for the level of experience of the individual.
- Feedback which is delivered inconsistently or negatively so that the individual either ignores it or dreads receiving it because it either lacks credibility or validity.

The solution is for the manager to ask quite specifically for feedback on how he delivers feedback and to adjust the nature and frequency of this accordingly.

Resource Gap the resource gap refers to the amount of resources available to carry out the performance requirements of the contract. As we saw in drawing up the support requirements, this is a difficult gap to review because of our natural inclination to want more resources than we get. Some forms of resource limitation provoke creativity; some inhibit creativity and with that, performance. Examining a resource gap requires more information – possibly historical information about the resource requirements of the work in the past and how these have changed for the future or a review of how competitors use resources. It also may involve a review of performance requirements if the resources cannot be made available to manage that part of the performance contract.

Authority gap a gap in authority results when there is an imbalance between the level of accountability and the authority required to carry out the requirements of that accountability. For example, when a manager is responsible for managing a team's performance and yet has no authority to recruit new members, review the organisation structure or arrange for team members to be rewarded for high performance. This happens regularly, particularly with first line management and creates many performance problems. It can happen at a higher level where an organisation devolves profit accountability to one of its strategic business units and yet retains control over pricing policy or the remuneration and benefit system.

The solution is to identify shortfalls in authority and work to rectify them. It may not always be possible to delegate authority formally but a satisfactory middle step may be a 'de facto' delegation of authority by the line manager whereby the subordinate inherits some of his manager's formal authority for use in certain situations even though it may require, for example, the 'sign-off' of the senior manager.

Motivation gap the motivation gap is the least tangible gap and, therefore, the one least susceptible to detailed analysis. A drop in motivation is often caused by one of the gaps referred to above. It is important to spend time with an individual to identify the cause of poor motivation and to try to place it in a more specific context so that a specific remedy can be applied. There are times, however, when their lack of commitment and motivation relates to something outside of work and the solution is for greater understanding on the part of the manager and a change in the balance of management behaviour.

Direction gap a direction gap occurs when an individual has some clear goals but is not sure how to achieve them. This may be due to a delegative management style misapplied to a less experienced person or it may be due to a confusion about the application of those goals into a particular organisational culture. A member of staff may think they know what to do but not be sure about how their approach will be perceived within the organisation. They may simply need some simple explanation about the boundaries of a decision they need to make. Probably the solution will be to explain and provide greater direction without taking the job back or robbing them of their freedom by giving too much direction too soon.

Reward gap the reward gap comes in two basic forms – the *remuneration gap* (not getting enough pay for the job) and the *recognition gap* (not getting enough recognition for high performance). These gaps are unlikely to arise during the diagnostic process unless the subordinate is either particularly frank about their pay or the manager is perceptive enough to pick up the signals. The recognition gap is more likely to create a performance problem. People are still likely, all other things being equal, to turn in good work even if they regard themselves as badly paid; without recognition, an extension of feedback, some staff are likely to feel like a comedian who gets no applause until the end of the act and clearly this must have an impact on their performance. It is important that the manager uses performance review and appraisals as a means of showing recognition and not just a purely rational means of passing on information about performance.

Barriers

The second set of causes of poor performance relate to barriers which organisations put in the way of individual performance. Instead of actually channelling people's energy, many organisations put barriers in the way of their staff and appear almost deliberately to prevent them from achieving their objectives. One of the first things that a manager must do to enhance the performance of staff is to think about some of the barriers that the organisation has created and work hard to remove them. In my experience these barriers fall into five different categories, some of which can be removed by the zealous action of the manager; some need the influence of people at the top of the organisation.

- **Functional:** Some very large barriers exist between departments and functions within organisations. It is almost as though people in different departments are actively working for the competition. In fact many people show less hostility towards their main business competitors than they do towards people in accounts or personnel or marketing. The cause of the functional barriers is sometimes the primitive territorial imperative which makes us mistrust people whom we regard as outside our tribe and restricts our comfort zone to those people who work in the same way as we do and who share our perspective. Whilst managers rarely create these barriers deliberately, it is essential that they work rapidly and effectively to remove them. People who focus on their own personal and professional agenda cannot be focused entirely on the business strategy of the organisation.

It is important, therefore, for organisations to ensure that all functions within the organisation are united behind the business strategy. The one key strategy which managers can pursue to help overcome functional barriers is to encourage the development of multi-disciplinary and cross-functional project teams, task forces and working parties. People who have worked together to achieve common project goals gain a new respect for the professional expertise of their colleagues and find it far more difficult to hide behind the old departmental prejudices once the project team has been broken up. Another way is to extend the concept of performance contracts into inter-departmental relationships, an issue that we will review in the next chapter.

- **Cultural:** Cultural barriers are those conventions and tribal myths which prevent things being done differently from the way they have been done in the past. All managers should have a healthy respect for culture and should work hard to emphasise those aspects of the corporate culture which bind people together and which create a positive feeling about the organisation, at the same time trying to break down those cultural and historical barriers which prevent people from doing things effectively. Managers need to manage organisational and team culture so that it ceases to become a brake on progress and becomes a spur to further achievement. It may be preventing people from trying new things and working in new ways which are important for the future development of the business.
- **Bureaucratic:** Readers who have taken part in total quality management programmes will be aware that one of the important aspects of this movement has been its emphasis on the reduction of bureaucratic barriers. Writers like C. Northcote Parkinson (*Parkinson's Law*, Penguin 1957) have written some very amusing articles about the folly of bureaucracy. Bureaucracy ceases to be amusing, however, when it becomes a web of red tape binding the limbs of the people who work within the organisation. There is clearly a need for order and routine within a large commercial organisation, but it should be minimised. Managers should examine all their working practices and processes to ensure that only those things which are essential to the achievement of the business strategy are being carried out. Far more than this, effective organisations have carried out campaigns against the

excessive use of paper. There is a need to review regularly all the processes within the organisation to ensure that unnecessary constraints and controls are being removed. A lot of this work should be done by managers within the organisation, who *must* model non-bureaucratic behaviour to the best of their ability – by not asking for information that they don't really need, not carrying out massive inspections on a whim and not treating people like potentially delinquent children – and by so doing remove some of the myriad of unnecessary checks and balances which operate within the organisation.

- **Status:** The first set of barriers, functional, related to lateral problems between colleagues in different departments. An even more insidious barrier to organisational performance is the problem of status. This happens when people within an organisation are denied their opportunity to make a full contribution because of perceptions of their status. These barriers may be imposed by other people in the organisation or they may be perceived by individuals themselves. Whatever the reason, they reduce individual contribution and therefore deny the organisation access to the full creativity of people within it. The organisation strategy under these circumstances must be twofold – 1) to reduce the levels of staff wherever possible and 2) to remove any visible symbols of status which may bolster up the flagging egos of senior people and damage the confidence and therefore the performance, of junior people.

  The line manager must fight hard to break down status barriers so that his or her staff are able to make their full contribution as equals and not be inhibited by their own and others perceptions of relative status.
- **Glass ceilings:** Glass ceilings are those invisible signals within an organisation that the contribution of certain categories of people are not likely to be as fully rewarded as the contributions of others. At the present time, this is particularly noticeable in terms of the development of women, ethnic minorities and the disabled within organisations. The glass ceiling is so called because it is not visible to anyone apart from the person whose head keeps bumping against it. In an organisation which claims to have full equal opportunities, the only people who would sense the glass ceiling would be the women who find it hard to break through that ceiling to get into higher grades of management. These glass ceilings will only be broken by the combined efforts of managers within the organisation and policy makers at the very top. Their effect is to denigrate the contribution of certain categories by denying them access to the more influential jobs within the organisation; this creates negative feelings in the minds of

the people who belong to that minority and inhibits their performance by devaluing their contribution.

The point about equal opportunity programmes is that they should provide equality of opportunities for all staff which in turn gives the organisation access to the full potential of the whole workforce. To appeal to the whole organisation for support in times of adversity and yet still, by inference, regard one group more favourably than another is a dilution of the whole organisation's potential for performance. Managers need to work at breaking down these barriers continuously, and particularly when the barriers are preventing *their* team, and therefore themselves, from fulfilling their performance contracts.

The causes of poor performance are legion. I have set out an analysis of gaps and barriers more to trigger thoughts in the reader's mind rather than to set down a definitive set of causes of performance problems. The important factor in solving performance problems is that the solution needs to be related to the cause, which can only be discovered by rigorous analysis on the part of both parties to the performance contract. The next important stage is implementation of the solution.

IMPLEMENTATION OF THE SOLUTION

This is again a joint process which needs to have some clear guidelines set out. Identifying the solution is only part of the issue, however, albeit a very important one. The implementation phase has three important objectives:

- To ensure that a jointly agreed action plan is produced to bring performance back on track.
- To verify that the agreed solution is actually the true cause of the problem.
- To build in some preventative measures in order to ensure that the problem does not recur.

The aim of the action planning process is to raise the performance in the unmet objective or objectives to the level required in the performance contract. This involves reviewing the whole performance contract by:

1. setting interim output and capability objectives in order to ensure that progression is gradual and constant. We return to the old dilemma of stretching versus achievable objectives. In a situation where new objectives have been introduced and so far not achieved, my advice would be to set slightly increased objectives but with more

regular reviews which would, in turn, translate the problem-solving loop into a continuous improvement process. The important element of this is the creation of a series of small successes and boosting confidence to enable a goal to be achieved and, as a consequence, being given something more to aim for as a result of those successes;
2. reviewing the levels of resource, authority and training/coaching in line with the reset objectives, particularly if a support gap has been identified in any of those areas;
3. slightly adjusting the management style to take this new element into account. We have already seen that in the situational leadership model, everybody requires some mixture of support and direction. In the case of experienced people, the mixture is more supportive; less experienced people require more direction. When performance problems occur, the manager needs to adjust the mixture slightly; not drastically but in small steps until the right balance is achieved. This again depends on the reason for the performance problem; if it is a competence gap, then the manager will certainly need to provide much more direction. If there is some other reason, the manager may need to provide some more support during the period of bringing performance back on track. The important factor is not to over-direct if this is not required, otherwise there will be a future performance issue developing quietly before the current one has gone away.

One further comment about the problem-solving process. I have stressed the need to avoid the woolly expression poor performance; there is an even greater need to avoid the expression 'poor performer'. The phrase has a terrible condemnatory effect on people in an organisation and may mean that they develop a credibility gap which prevents them from performing effectively in the organisation ever again. We do, however, have to face the fact that certain people in certain jobs have chronic performance problems and occasionally we also come across an acute performance problem. These situations still need to go through the problem-solving cycle that I have just described, at least initially. It can happen that a performance problem in one critical success factor can have a domino effect in another area particularly if it is a critical issue. We may be able to resolve chronic 'below standard' performance across the range by resolving one important issue.

However, if we have worked through all the elements of the performance contract and still not resolved the problem, we may have to ask some more searching questions:

- **The job/person 'fit'** – do we have the right person in the right job? Are they new to the job or has their job grown in one direction whilst they have grown in the other? Do we change the person, redesign the job or agree an action plan to ensure the two fit together better?

- **The company/person 'fit'** – do we have the right person in the right organisation? Does the culture affect their performance and would they do better outside the organisation?
- **Physical problems** – are there some physical problems which make the job difficult – long hours, travelling, recovering from illness? Are drink or drugs problems affecting performance and if so, what deeper issues do they conceal?
- **Working conditions** – is the working environment conducive to high performance? Is it too noisy/crowded/potentially unsafe/badly designed?
- **Personal issues** – are there domestic problems, either long- or short-term? Are there personality issues with other colleagues or other departments? Building good relationships with a particular section should be one of the capability objectives in the contract if it is sufficiently important.

These issues and the many more which may contribute to performance problems are outside the direct remit of the performance contract but they need to be addressed if they are barriers to performance. The first role of the manager is to support – ask open questions, listen carefully and probe gently. These are the actions of a supportive friend; the actions that we would all ask of our boss under similar circumstances. The second stage may be to ask for professional support; your personnel manager is the best person to call on. Welfare is no longer part of the personnel role: performance counselling is an increasing part but only after the line manager has done a lot of problem-analysis with the individual. The performance contract does not involve the personnel manager; it is between manager and subordinate. In 99 per cent of cases, problems which arise can be resolved by the two people who have the most interest in their resolution.

So far, discipline has not been discussed. Discipline is still part of the performance contract; our boss still has some power to coerce us to conform if we fail to agree on a contract. It is, however, a defeat: a sad admission on the part of both parties that they cannot agree on a set of performance and support requirements to make an effective contract between them. If the contract process, performance reviews and performance counselling all fail, then the disciplinary process should be gone through in line with the company's procedures. The disciplinary process is the same as the process we have just reviewed but with a judicial perspective supported by sanctions. In my experience of many disciplinary hearings, they never seem to resolve those issues which cannot be resolved at work. Like the divorce procedure, the adversarial nature of the process focuses attention, not on repairing the marriage but on concluding who was to blame for the breakdown. Few working relationships recover completely from that.

The performance contract does have some similarities to marriage. It is a relationship based on trust from which both parties should benefit. If it starts to break down, there are few better alternative remedies than a frank discussion on what is going wrong – both side wanting to resolve the issue; both sides respecting each other's rights.

11

Performance Contracts Throughout the Organisation

The process of drawing up contracts is well established between organisations but relatively unknown within them. For example, one of the important issues raised in relation to total quality management has been the relationship between customers and suppliers within organisations and this too lends itself to the contracting process.

The basis of the performance contract is between the manager and the individual. The first issue in relation to spreading the contracts is the need to give coherence to the whole team's work and to put it in the context of the work of the organisation.

THE CONCEPTS OF MISSION AND VISION

There are two important elements of performance management which need to be carried out both by people at the top of an organisation and managers throughout the organisation. Two words which have become slightly jaded by over-use, but which represent concepts which are critical if the organisation is to achieve its strategic objectives, are 'vision' and 'mission'. However well managed and well organised the company or unit is, they need to have direction and they need to understand the meaning of the work they carry out. This gives coherence to the work done on individual performance contracts by putting it into a wider context. Effective organisations have already discovered this and have emphasised the importance of these two concepts as a co-ordinating force and used them to replace complex policy and procedural manuals.

One of the most remarkable changes in the workplace over the last fifteen to twenty years has been the increase in desire for greater levels of responsibility by the workers. At one time it was sufficient to provide people with very clear and detailed guidance on what they should do and how they should do it. Now there is a strong desire on the part of most people to do work which has some meaning and in which they can see themselves making a valuable and unique contribution to both the organisation and the society which it serves. One of the effects of greater organisational delegation which has resulted in splitting up parts of the organisation into semi-autonomous units has been the need to find some sort of cement to bind the organisation, albeit loosely, to a common corporate goal.

The first responsibility of the organisation is to clarify their mission. Putting 'mission' in the context of our performance model, it becomes the set of strategic objectives or desired outcomes. They are the things that we are here to do – increase profit, sales, customer satisfaction, reduce labour turnover, improve quality of life, better education and so on. They are not just the outputs – the things that we create – but they are the raison d'etre of the organisation, literally the reason for its existence.

Mission statements need to answer the questions 'what' and 'why'. They need to be more than a slogan thought up by either a management consultant or an advertising agency; beneath the words of a mission statement there needs to be a strong sense of purpose. This is a key role of the management within an organisation: the statement and clarification of purpose for their working group. Organisational mission statements are important and potentially inspirational, but they need to be underpinned by purposeful statements defining the roles of departments, functions, units, regiments and so on. It may be exciting to know that Trans Global Chemicals aims to be the biggest and most innovative polymer manufacturer in the world – but how does that inspire the small team of plant cleaners in their Macclesfield factory? They need to know why they are there and how they can support this ambitious global thrust. Effective organisations break their mission statements down into critical success factors and cascade these throughout the organisation. The mission should be reviewed regularly with information on actual outcomes so that there is a sense of continuous improvement driven by feedback from either the outside world or the relevant internal customers.

The mission is to do with today's performance. My dictionary defines it as 'a specific task or duty assigned to a person or group of people'. However, if it is to be a completely effective motivator it needs to be linked with a sense of vision – a sense of how the operation can be developed in the future. A clear view of the future communicated to the organisation and supported by measurable improvements in the infrastructure can be very effective in confirming that there is an exciting future and that the organisation is equipped to meet it. Without a sense of future direction each mission becomes an end in itself with no real incentive to strive for constant and continuous improvement and development. The aim of continuous improvement and development is to set the organisation on a course which takes both performance and development onto a constantly rising level – it needs to be set clearly and to be something more exciting and meaningful than achieving this year's targets.

Vision is not just needed at the strategic level within the organisation; it is not the preserve of 'clever people at Head Office'. It should be part of the role of every manager – to be alert to a changing environment, tuned in to customer requirements or a changing legal framework, in short, to be thinking about the changing role for the organisation in the future.

During the recent reforms in the National Health Service, particularly the introduction of the internal market, I ran, with a colleague, a seminar for consultant paediatricians on the changing environment and their role within it. I was struck by the dichotomy between those who had foreseen the changes and were happily adapting to them, and those who had not foreseen them and were desperately reacting to them. Any of the first category would have managed more effectively, even if the legislation had not finally been passed, because they were sensing the external environment and converting their perception into real tasks and action plans. Darwin taught us that in a process of evolution, adaptability is a predictor of survival. Prescience, the gift of foresight, is an important factor in adapting to a new environment. The effective management of performance involves understanding the direction for the future and then steering enthusiastically towards it.

Concepts like mission and vision draw a groan from many a practising line manager who see them as woolly concepts thought up by people with filofaxes and cellular telephones. Of course, left alone they are. In order to be fully effective they need to be supported by clear and measurable standards of output and this becomes the responsibility of the manager within the organisation – the conversion of mission and visionary statements into performance contracts which can be put into effect by people within the organisation.

MISSIONS AND VISIONS: MAKING THEM HAPPEN

Essentially there are five processes which an organisation needs to go through both to create a vision for the future, to ensure that the organisation is committed to it, to convert it into a mission statement, and to be implementing and putting it under continuous review.

Creating the vision

A vision of the future comes in many different forms. People at the top of the organisation need to have a much longer term vision than people at the bottom. The size and structure of the modern organisation takes time to effect the necessary change in strategy and culture which a new business environment requires. This is not to say that vision should be the monopoly of senior people. Department managers, section managers and other line managers need to be equally visionary but their horizon, because they are further down the organisation, may itself be slightly nearer. The people at the top should be able to see much further. The vision of where an organisation is going should be created by the people at the top, not necessarily as a consultative process. To be consultative at this stage is like saying 'Does anybody know where we are heading?'. Great leaders are normally people with great vision – either a vision of the future and how it may change or a vision on how some huge current problem can be overcome. They may, however, want to enlist the support of people within the organisation, encouraging them to be acutely aware of their environment and to feed back into the organisation any signs that they have of significant changes in the business environment.

Sharing the vision

The next process is the sharing and communicating of the vision amongst the organisation as a whole. This is one of the most important roles which a management team needs to fulfil and they need to be working on that constantly as one of their main priorities. Too often the corporate strategy, which is normally a more detailed and boring version of the organisation's vision, is kept very secret because of the fear of it's falling into the hands of competitors. However, organisations who keep secret their vision of the future miss a trick in relation to their own staff. It is not always the quality of the vision which creates the competitive edge, it is often the way it is shared and communicated amongst the organisation.

Communicating your corporate vision is something which needs to be done simply, but with enthusiasm. It should consist of defining exciting and challenging concepts in a simple and visual way. The most successful communicators have worked on extending and enhancing their natural style rather than bringing in speech writers and image creators to polish up their speeches. People who work in organisations are very sensitive to insincerity and a phony, anodyne statement of the future will inspire nobody; whereas an unpolished but inspirational message about your own individual vision will bring people together behind you.

Converting vision into mission

Converting the vision into a mission is the first stage of getting it achieved. The organisation needs to know what it is expected to do; a set of outcomes for which it is striving. This goes all the way from the top of the organisation down and a key role of the manager is converting values, customer needs and legal requirements into individual and team missions. A concrete statement of what the organisation is here to do today will help it find its way to the slightly more evanescent vision of the future. People at the top of the organisation have to be able to translate their message into terms which actually set the output targets for the whole organisation and help turn the statements into action.

Implementing the mission

Implementing the mission is what everyone in the organisation is there to do. The manager's contribution is the creation of appropriate organisation structures and the development of people so that they can achieve the mission targets of the organisation. Something that the top team and all managers in the organisation can do is to carry out a process which is known as 'zooming'. By this we mean to imitate the action of the expensive camera, which can zoom in from taking a broad scenic shot to taking a close shot of something very specific and very detailed. Managers at the top of large organisations often keep themselves permanently at a strategic level and regard themselves as strategists and visionaries. They need, however, to move sometimes from the strategic and visionary to the operational and specific very quickly in order to ensure that the things that they say *should* happen within the organisation *do* happen, and to a standard that they regard as appropriate for their organisation.

The chairman of the chemical company who asks for an explanation of an oil leak on the factory floor, the director of a food retail company who is in the stores regularly checking their appearance and stock availability are practising zooming, moving from the strategic to the operational. This has a number of important consequences:

- It enables them to see exactly what is going on within their own organisation.
- It gives a very strong message to the organisation as a whole that effective implementation and execution is as important as thinking up bold strategic plans.
- It demonstrates a knowledge and an interest in the way things are done right the way through the organisation.

Reviewing the mission

Change is now too turbulent to enable leisurely strategic reviews of the organisation on an annual basis. There is a need to keep a constant eye on the environment and on the results of a whole range of issues which the organisation regards as strategic. Measurement is the first imperative in terms of ensuring that the organisation's strategic objectives are still appropriate. The targets within the organisation need to be set and reviewed on a rolling basis, ie the organisation's vision and mission should be reviewed regularly. They should also be the basis of all the other things that the organisation carries out, and each function's vision and mission statements should be consonant with the total organisation strategy. Functions like personnel, information technology, marketing and finance should all have their own vision and mission which dovetails in with that of the organisation. Their functional heads should equally be men and women of vision within their own function, as well as people who can participate in the work of the business as a whole.

Creating a sense of vision and mission within the organisation is critical to the effective operation of performance contracts. Without corporate direction in the wider sense, the contracts would still be appropriate for the manager and individual but would lack a coherence throughout the organisation. By proclaiming the organisation's mission, the top team are clarifying the guiding principle for all the performance contracts within the organisation; by communicating the organisation's vision, the top team are saying 'This is where we are heading, make sure that your performance contracts reflect that and include objectives that take us towards that goal'.

INTERNAL MARKETS

A further feature of an effective performance contract process and one which augments and supports performance contracts is a system of internal contracts between suppliers and customers *within* the organisation. The organisation is not only operating in a marketplace, it is in itself a large internal market with people supplying goods and services to each other across the organisation. This concept of the internal market is important insofar as it makes people aware of their relationship with others and how that relationship ultimately supports the organisation's offer to the external customer.

Some organisations have gone further than others in formalising the internal relationships between supplier and customer. The recent reforms in the National Health Service have created a dichotomy between service commissioners and service providers, and created free movement within the market, so that commissioners and providers not only negotiate the levels of service and the cost, they also have the freedom to explore other alternative providers if they find services and costs uncompetitive. This is an unlikely possibility between units and departments in most organisations – the suppliers are generally monopoly suppliers. We are unlikely to be in a position where we can consult another accounts department or another personnel department for support. There are, however, a series of creative options – sub-contracting, out-sourcing for services such as training in competition with in-house departments and a straightforward system of internal charging for services.

Having operated in a variety of systems, I prefer to concentrate on an internal performance cycle between suppliers and customers within the organisation. This cycle should form the basis of a relationship which can move in any direction that the organisation wishes at a later stage. As with the performance contract between manager and individual, I believe that the contractual relationship should be established first before adding any financial element to it. The National Health Service is suffering from this at the moment. The contractual relationships, forged under the pressure of financial constraints and publicity, have not had time to mature and develop.

The process of lateral performance contracting needs to be established with some quite simple objectives before moving on further. The importance of establishing a contractual relationship is that functions develop a partnership by instituting a free and open exchange of expectations and setting these down in a form of contract. As with the manager/employee contract, there are two sides to the process – the internal customer has obligations as well as rights, although the main thrust of the contract is the execution of the performance requirements. Each part of the performance cycle has its place in the internal market between customer and supplier.

Output (or service) objectives

This is the simple clarification of the level of service required and offered across the range of the supplier's and customer's critical success factors. This may focus on several critical success factors or one key area. For example, the personnel function will almost certainly provide a broad-ranging service to every other department across the whole of their own critical success factors; for example:

- Recruitment
- Remuneration and benefits
- Staff development and training
- Advice and support to line management
- Personnel information systems

The service objectives would also include elements which need to be maintained, improved and developed as well as those parts of the current service which are no longer required.

Capability objectives

The set of supporting objectives – those which help develop systems, skills, structures and assets – are also critical in the customer/supplier relationship. What do we need to be working on in order to enhance our relationship and our joint performance in the future? In the personnel contract, we may agree to run a series of training programmes on customer care this year as a service objective, but to conduct a detailed training needs analysis for the sales division during the year in order to review training needs for the next year as a capability objective.

Support requirements

The customer cannot get off lightly in the contract, at least not the internal contract. Within the internal contract, the customer has some support requirements to agree:

- **Resources** – what resources am I prepared to give to my supplier in terms of information, money, machinery, time (my own people's time) and systems?
- **Authority** – how will we agree on the balance of authority and accountability between the functions? For example, as an operations director, am I prepared to concede the personnel director any authority over wage levels, recruitment decisions and attendance on training programmes? If I concede no authority, then the personnel function has no accountability for these elements and I become fully accountable for areas over which I have little experience. If, however, I concede too much authority, the personnel function is going to be running quite significant areas of my operation for me and that may give me some problems. In the end the decision will need to be agreed and contracted for; it may be that there is a long-term process of lateral delegation from so-called support functions to the line managers. The responsibility for recruitment may now rest with personnel but it may

be agreed that the process will be delegated to line managers over a period of time after the appropriate training and, in the manner of situational leadership, reducing the amount of direction but maintaining some support.

- **Training and development** – what does the supplier need to know about my needs and my business in order to enhance the service he gives to me? The customer has to state his needs clearly but should also educate the supplier in the main elements of their business.

Performance review

The contract should be reviewed regularly at three levels of review – good, on the spot feedback; a regular formal review of the main elements of the contract and a long-term development review where the nature of the relationship is discussed and the future needs of the customer and supplier reviewed in the light of the organisation's long-term development.

Continuous Improvement

The continuous improvement cycle is critical to the effective customer/supplier relationship. The first performance contract sets down the basis of the performance and support requirements but this should be enhanced at every opportunity, particularly at every review. The achievement of one service level should be the trigger, if necessary, to work out some way of enhancing it and include this in the revised service contract.

Problem-solving

The failure to meet a particular service objective should provoke a joint problem-solving exercise and a complete review of the whole contract. Almost all the gaps which are apparent at an individual level become apparent at a departmental or functional level – capability gaps (not knowing enough about the business), appraisal gaps (not getting enough high quality feedback), authority gaps (not being allowed the authority to achieve objectives) and the gaps covered in Chapter 10 can all be reasons for failure to meet requirements.

The basis of the inter-departmental relationships within an organisation should, therefore, be the performance contract, which is, effectively the same thing as the contract between manager and individual. The organisation can build up a network of contracts between its functions and departments as well as a cascade of networks between managers and subordinates. There is, however, one final group of contracts that needs to be reviewed – those of projects going on throughout the organisation.

Project management

The need to improve project management skills within organisations is a further critical component of effective performance management. The process of contracting for performance and other management disciplines can support the effective introduction of new projects – an increasingly important element of the work of organisations today. We can identify two sorts of work in organisations – steady state work and project work. Steady state work is the day-to-day management of the business and project work is the introduction of new systems, products, procedures or technologies. We have already identified the need to maintain the philosophy of continuous improvement with regard to steady state work; the work of project management is to ensure that the other type of improvement, innovation, is managed and introduced as skilfully as possible and fitted in to the day-to-day operation of the organisation.

There are several reasons why project management is becoming more important:

- The increasing pace of technological and managerial change. Changes cannot now just be allowed to drift in, they need to be identified and implemented rapidly in order for the organisation to retain its competitive edge.
- Increasing complexity of modern business organisations has created the need to bring together more functions in relation to business projects. Organisations are now developing into networks of people who may have no formal organisational connection but who are nevertheless interdependent. Also, many people find that they no longer always work for one person and that their working life consists of a series of projects loosely based around a core of steady state work. As organisations become more complex, the need to harness the activity of a greater number of people accentuates the importance of effective project management and so far from mere administrative neatness, project management is becoming an important way of bringing people and activities together.
- An extension of this is the increase in horizontal management. Project managers need to work hard to bring together the work of people for whom they have no line authority. This can only be done if there are clear guidelines on how the project should be managed and if performance contracts are clarified at an early state.

- The introduction of new products and new technology is seen as increasingly high risk. The complexity of some business projects involves very high risk of failure and effective project management is necessary to ensure that these risks are minimised and that appropriate contingencies are put in place. Because of the pressurised nature of projects, this can only be done by effective performance management so that the risks are managed rather than avoided.

There are three key areas of a project in which performance management needs to be examined – performance management, risk assessment and project handover.

Performance management

The inception phase of a project is there to test the viability of the original proposal and to put together the components of a successful project. Effective organisations take proposals and examine their feasibility by running a *pilot* or *feasibility project* at an early stage. It is no longer possible to put together a very detailed plan and wait until every component is in place before going ahead. One of the important issues which *In Search of Excellence* and its successors have raised has been the concept of 'ready, fire, aim' whereby an organisation launches a new project in pilot form and then reviews its effectiveness quickly rather than waiting longer for a new project to achieve conceptual perfection before any sort of trial or pilot. Once a project has been tested and given the go ahead, then there is a need to create a clear performance contract and appoint a team to manage the project. That team should consist of a project director, a project manager and a series of specialists who will tackle sub-projects within the wider framework.

The planning of a project demands effective performance management. The following needs must be established:

- clear definition of the performance required of the project team agreed with the sponsors;
- clear definition of the support which will be given to the project team;
- agreement on when performance and targets should be reviewed;
- agreement on the systems which will be available to support the measurement of the project's success;
- how changes in the nature of the project will be identified and introduced;
- how the project will communicate its progress to interested parties.

This is where the disciplines of performance management become relevant to the disciplines of project management. The project manager will need to put together a measurable project plan which should be agreed by all members of the project team. It is not within the scope of this book to define how this should be done and there are a number of well-tried techniques to support the planning and development of projects. It is, however, critical that the plan is credible (ie it contains the right activities and has been discussed with all interested parties), that it is manageable (ie it has check points and milestones which can be attained by the project team and supported by management information systems) and thirdly that it is acceptable (agreed to by all members of the project team and members of the wider audience of people who will be affected by the work that is carried out). The project plan becomes an extension of the performance management cycle. It also needs to be translated into individual contracts so that each individual understands exactly what is required of them in the project. This is particularly important as project teams are quite often dispersed physically and so need a clear idea of the direction of the overall project and their role in it before they go back to work on their chunk of the project.

Risk assessment

Risk assessment is an important part of the project manager's role. Risks should be assessed on both the impact that they would create and the probability of them happening. Initially, the project manager and the project team should draft out a number of things which could put the project at risk in a major or a minor sense. At a later stage they should go through each of these to assess them in terms of impact and probability. Risk should be reviewed as part of the management contract and the people who are the end users of the project should be consulted and be fully aware of the risks that may occur so that they can identify the impact and explain whether that level of risk is acceptable to them.

Project handover

The aim of a project is to transfer the end product into a satisfactory operational environment and this is often the most difficult part of the project management role. It is difficult for a number of reasons – the main one is that a successful team hates to break up and there is a tendency to hold on to the project for longer than necessary. A further problem is that the level of understanding of people within the organisation probably will not have the deep specialist knowledge that members of the project team have developed. Their role, however, is to convert the project work into a normal operating environment and a good project handover should be a seamless transfer of work from the high pressurised project environment into the routine of steady state work.

A key factor in this is, of course, the training and development of people who are responsible for managing the work on a day-to-day basis. The basic rules of delegation apply here and this classic example of the importance of lateral delegation should be tackled on the basis of the well-tried situational leadership model, in which the project team gives a lot of direction and guidance at first, slowly handing over authority to the people who are responsible for doing the work on a daily basis. The project should also be monitored regularly, with the project manager or one of the team retaining evaluating responsibility for the project rather than allowing the whole thing to disband rapidly.

We now have a range of different contracts which run through the whole organisation – boss/subordinate, inter-departmental, and project. The next stage is to examine:

- how these contracts interact;
- how the process can be carried out without creating a huge bureaucracy;
- how the process can be introduced;
- how the contracting process may develop in the future.

How do the contracts interact?

Potentially, we have a complex web of performance contracts across and around the organisation. There are several mechanisms that have already been reviewed which should help ensure that contracts interact positively:

- A clear sense of mission, so that people are clear about the direction of the organisation.
- Close relationships between functions and a mutual understanding of each other's purpose and mission.
- The use of contracts in project management.
- The process of cascading contracts.

The model that we have in the organisation looks like Figure 17.

The contracts interact in an apparently complex way but not if they start from the top of the organisation and work down. The board needs to formulate the organisation's mission, then each board director will agree a performance contract with the chief executive officer. The process should then move down to heads of function or heads of department. This is probably the most effective stage of starting the process of agreeing lateral contracts across departments for suppliers and customers. This should, I believe, be initiated by suppliers who will use the information gathered in their discussion with their customers to set and clarify the

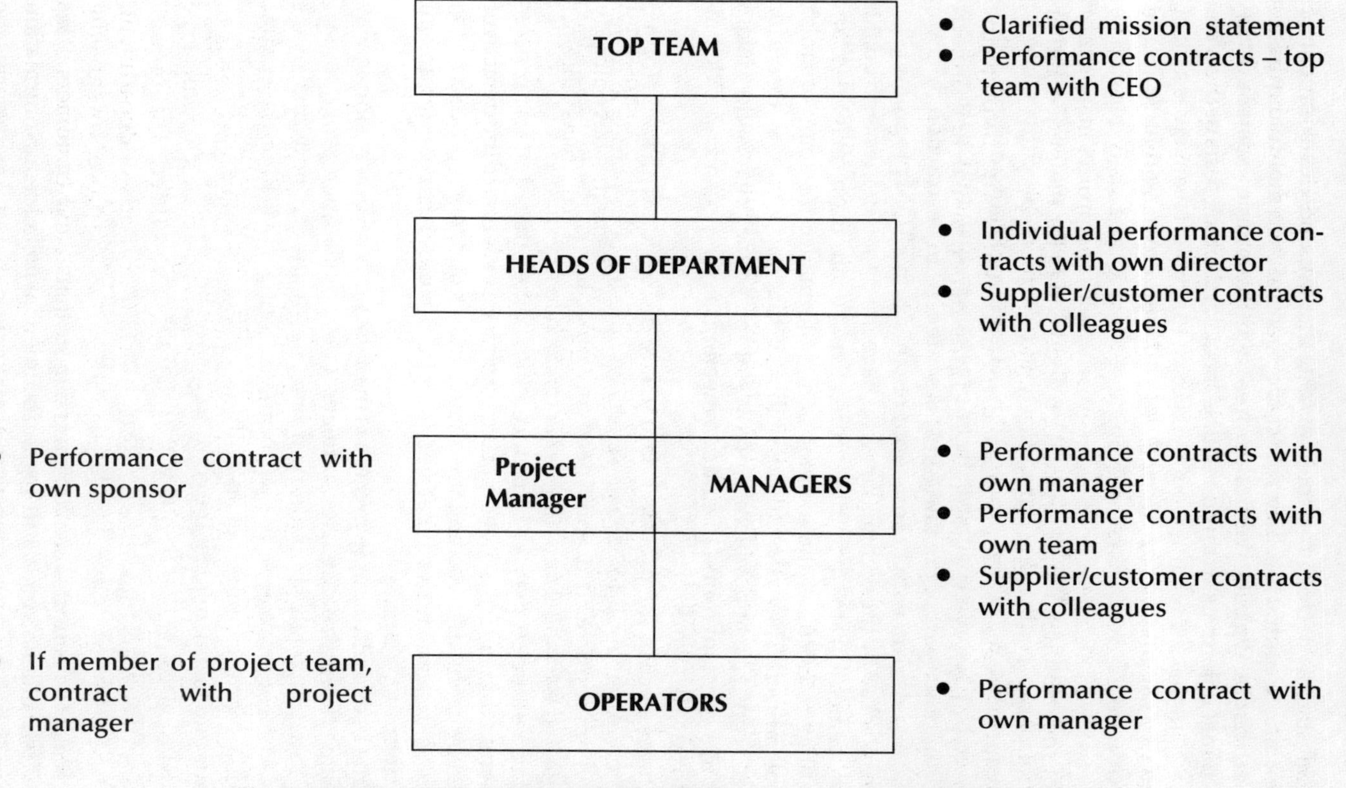

Figure 17 *Organisational model for performance contract interaction*

critical success factors for their own team. This creates a system of performance contracts which reflect the needs of the whole organisation rather than a typically vertical process which tends to sustain purely functional objectives without relating them across the business.

How can the process be carried out without creating a huge bureaucracy?

There is a, quite justifiable, fear in the minds of many managers that the 'performance contracting' process should be more properly named a 'bureaucracy expanding' process! It has that terrible aura of a procedure devised by personnel people to tie line managers up in ribbons of red tape while another part of the rain forest is sentenced to destruction. Many of us have looked on with horror as our organisation's TQM programme has been hijacked by the commissars who have filled their diaries with quality improvement team meetings, corrective action team meetings and meetings to calculate the price of non-conformance for some organisational project. They see the possibility of this happening with performance contracts and a picture unfolds of the whole organisation taking part in a constant round of contract meetings until we can find little time to do any real work.

The essence of the process is face to face discussion with some form of written explanation to act as a reference note for both parties to review when appropriate. It doesn't need any other forms; the process I have suggested is a model and may be customised to fit your own organisation and its culture. It may be introduced into some other strategic process, although there is the danger that it may significantly dilute the objectives. It can be useful in preceding the organisation's budgeting process so that there is a clear idea of what needs to be done before costings are put together.

This essentially simple process is managed in a relatively simple way. Even if, as we shall see later, it relates to a remuneration programme, it can be a completely straightforward process – either an individual meets, fails to meet or exceeds the performance contract. Meeting the contract qualifies for the bonus, consistently exceeding the contract gets a bigger bonus and failing to meet the contract gets no bonus at all. This may seem stark but it shows that it can be made simple – although the organisation may have valid reasons for making it more complex.

A few tips when drawing up a performance contract:

- Make the performance contract no more than two or three sides of A4. It should not be a full legal document with addenda, errata and codicils. A clear, measurable statement of the key elements of performance required and the support required to achieve them should not look like the first draft of *The Brothers Karamazov*.

- Agree the nature of the measures and try, where possible, to use similar measures at each review, hopefully with different numbers against them. This economises on time at the review session. You should, however, carry out a periodic 'blank paper' exercise when you write up the contract as if for the first time. This encourages people to take a fresh look at the job.
- Don't go into either negotiating or 'appraisal' mode. The performance contract is a win-win process; both sides have to come out successfully otherwise they both fail. In my experience, a manager going to a director to explain a failure to meet their requirements will not get far by explaining how a member of their team let them down in failing to achieve their objectives.

How should the process be introduced?

The drafting of the initial performance contracts is the most difficult and time-consuming part of the exercise. There is no doubt that for many organisations it is a new and quite daunting process which takes some time to accommodate into the normal, already busy life of the company. Instead of looking at how to introduce it effectively, it may be more interesting to look at some ways of introducing it *in*effectively:

- **Introduce it throughout the whole organisation at once.** That is, top down and laterally and ensure that the introduction process is worked out on a tight deadline. As we know, introducing new concepts on a tight deadline has the effect of concentrating the mind and also gets the whole process in place quickly.
- **Try to avoid complicated explanations about the process.** The process is simple; your managers are intelligent so it is very likely that they will pick it up fairly quickly in their own idiosyncratic way.
- **Encourage the personnel department to introduce the programme and monitor it carefully.** Performance contracts should be drafted on a form designed for the process, with copies sent to the manager's boss and the personnel department, perhaps with a copy for the personal file as well so that the department can keep track of performance improvement.
- **Tie the contracting process into some sort of remuneration planning process as soon as possible**. This has a tremendous effect on the tone of the process – it tends to make people far more collaborative when they become aware that the results of the discussion, or negotiation, can result in increased payments to them with, possibly, the minimum of effort.

- **Announce the process some time in advance**, (particularly if it involves financial gain). It ensures that people hold back any possible personal productivity improvement until the contracts are introduced; this ensures that the whole idea has a tremendous start.

Regrettably, these are some real issues that organisations have gone through to introduce performance contracts. They are also the problems which occurred with performance appraisal. Performance management is a significant cultural change which requires careful introduction and a period of settling in until the organisation and the people within it are comfortable with the process. Only at this stage can the remuneration element be introduced without fear of distorting the performance contract.

A further point is that contracts should be initially fairly simple – with 'outcome' measures and some easily measurable outputs. They are likely to become more sophisticated as they develop but managers would be wise not to aim for too much sophistication until they have fully understood the contracting process.

How the contracting process may develop in the future?

I believe that the process of agreeing formal contracts will be an important feature in any organisation of the future. People have changed in the last few years and the concept of management by command is becoming increasingly inappropriate. As performance contracts become established, the major change will be related to the change in organisation structures – this is already happening and will be a feature of the 'ad-hocratic' organisation of the future. We shall be examining organisation structures later – but briefly, the old pyramidal structures are already breaking down and creating a structure, more like that shown in Figure 18.

The person covered by box A will have at least two, if not more, relationships – a functional relationship and one or more project or product relationships. The likelihood is, as the pace of change increases, that most people will find themselves in a variety of authority relationships in an organisation. This may be complicated by an increase in subcontracting out of some non-core elements of the organisation's work.

The consequence of this fluidity in organisational design will be the breakdown of the simple relationship between the manager and subordinate – the relationship upon which the performance contract is based. This change may produce a shift from the contract process cascading down the organisation to one in which the individual holds and manages a series of performance contracts for which they are accountable. This

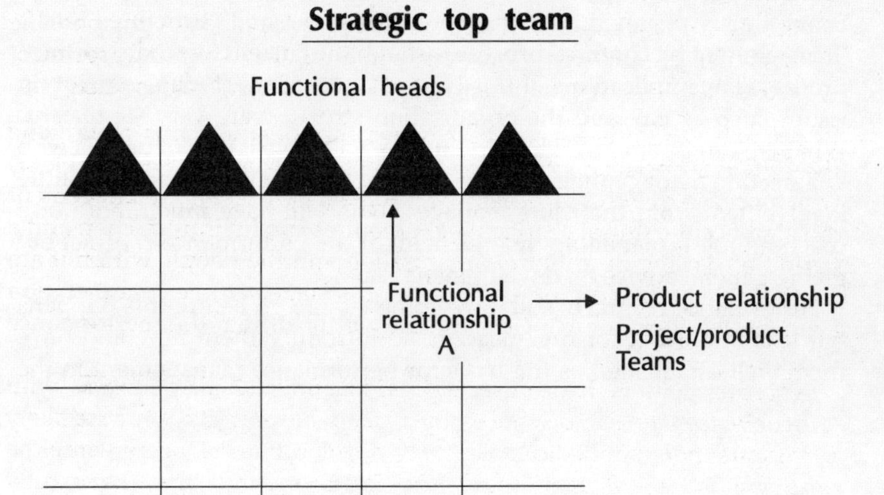

Figure 18 *The development of organisational structures*

may not apply to absolutely everyone in the organisation, for people producing basic outputs and services are likely to continue to do this as they do at present. It will, however, mean that the professional and managerial core of the organisation may be faced with a series of contracts to be managed. This is an extension of the status quo, but a more formalised extension than the majority of organisations are currently working to.

A situation could be envisaged where a research and development manager in a centralised research laboratory has the following set of contracts:

1. With the research and development director for the management of the laboratory and the people within it as well as the maintenance of professional standards.
2. With the product development director of the organisation for the development of new products to meet the company's marketing plan.
3. With the project manager of a new IT expert system on product testing for liaison between the project team and the end-user departments.
4. With the technical training director for the introduction of a new laboratory training programme for graduate chemists.

The process could go on longer, but the likelihood is that we will be converting our previous 'management by command' structures into a 'management by contract' process through the current 'cascade contract' process. The implications of this type of multi-contract management on issues such as pay and the organisation structure are very significant. What we can be sure of is that in time we will have layers of people who will need to manage their own performance and development with little involvement from their line manager, who will have much more of a coaching role – managing their element of the performance contract but giving general advice on development issues.

Performance contracts still have some way to go before this happens but it is important for organisations to introduce them now and have them well-established as the basis for performance management in the future.

12

The Continuous Development of People

Up to now we have focused on the performance cycle for the management of individual performance and in the last chapter explored how the performance cycle could be applied throughout the organisation. It is now time to review what the organisation needs to do to create a climate which supports the performance management process. The organisation will only enhance the performance management cycle when all of its human resource policies are working in the same direction – encouraging high performance and discouraging poor or mediocre performance.

There are five strategically important policies which need to be in place in order to support the achievement of individual and organisational performance goals:

- **Renewal** – the continuous development of people and renewal of the organisation's capability.
- **Restructuring** – the process by which the organisation constantly reviews its structure to ensure that it remains appropriate.
- **Recruitment** – the way that high performers are attracted towards the organisation.
- **Retention** – the way that those high performers are retained by the organisation.
- **Reward** – the process by which people are rewarded for their achievements.

The first element of this organisational climate is the renewal of the organisation's capability, particularly as it relates to the continuous development of individuals. The development of individual competence is an issue which demands the co-ordinated effort of the whole organisation in achieving this key activity. In my experience there are four important groups of people who need to come together to create what has become known as a 'learning organisation'. Each of these groups needs to be active in ensuring that people within the organisation get the development they need in order to enable the organisation to meet not only today's mission but also tomorrow's strategy. The four groups are:

1. Top management – The top management team have a great responsibility to encourage a high rate of organisational learning and to ensure that training and development is managed as a business activity and not as some form of social service. Attitudes manifested by the top team are soon taken up by the people who report to them and any insincerity in the commitment to the development of people will be sensed by other managers in the organisation. The anodyne statement in the Report and Accounts that 'our people are our greatest asset' needs to be supported by an active commitment in terms of time and resource.
2. Training and development professionals – Effective training and development specialists are essential if the most appropriate training and development is to be given. This is no longer related to people who can run a series of standard management courses; it requires specialists with a wide understanding of how people develop and the ability to influence the way things are done in the organisation. This means putting people with high potential into the development function and not people who are either failed managers or just happen to be 'good with people'. Highly effective development specialists can play a key role in the development of organisational capability; ineffective development professionals contribute little to the organisation apart from providing a few training courses and operational manuals.
3. Line managers – We have already identified the importance of the line manager's role as coach to their team. The development of fresh skills is as important a task for the line manager as the management of day-to-day performance; as I hope I have demonstrated, the two tasks are inextricably linked – we cannot do one effectively without doing the other. The manager as coach is a particularly relevant sporting analogy – the sporting coach is normally not an active performer and is off the pitch or court observing and encouraging, and then feeding these observations back to the performer in a way that encourages further growth and development. To be an effective coach, the manager needs to see this as a key role and give quality time to coaching by concentrating on the work of subordinates, observing and listening, before giving effective feedback when the job has been done.

4. Individuals – The most effective development comes from inside the individual. External influences – coach, mentor, trainer, director – can only create the environment and set the direction for development, but the motivation for personal development must come from within. In many organisations I sense a feeling from many employees that they are waiting to have some training or development 'done' to them – a passive approach on their part. This has to change; organisations must encourage people to take more responsibility for their own training and development, to state clearly how they want to be developed, to agree with their manager what training and development needs they have in order to meet their performance contracts. These are active tasks in which the individual has as much right to be involved as their manager or trainer.

Each of these four factors needs to be present if an organisation is to be effectively developing competence within their people and can be examined.

THE ROLE OF TOP MANAGEMENT

The senior management team within an organisation have a critical role to play in the continuous development of the organisation. They must take seriously their own training and development both individually and as part of a management team. They should also identify successors and help to prepare them for moving into the top jobs. Carrying out these two activities in themselves would have a huge impact on the way the organisation operates. Much of the evidence gathered by people like Professor Alan Mumford is that directors tend to emerge within the organisation and suddenly find themselves in one of the top strategic roles within an organisation with very little preparation. The key job is often filled with least preparation.

These two activities, developing the top team and developing their successors, can only be effectively co-ordinated by directors themselves. Other professionals within the organisation can contribute with their own professional expertise, but only someone who has operated at a board level can hope to oversee fully the development of their successors. The board of directors should co-ordinate this activity but they must utilise fully the resources available to them both within their own organisation (particularly their own training and development professionals) and outside specialists such as business schools or consultancy organisations. The accountability for the development of both themselves and their successors is too important to either ignore or to delegate completely to other people.

Furthermore, those resources must be evaluated regularly. Training is not a process that can be carried out on the cheap: it needs to be supported by an appropriate level of resource. The top team should be looking for a return from those training resources and should be evaluating, actively and critically, the outcomes. Training and development is a function much given to blurring edges and it needs to be rigorously evaluated to ensure that it is still providing the training and development that the organisation needs. Earlier we saw that learning related to change and that one of the skills of the learning organisation was to keep in touch with the environment. Directors have an important responsibility to act as a bridge between the environment and the organisation. They need to be scanning the commercial horizon regularly, looking five to ten years ahead and converting that information into development plans for the future. Directors are well placed to carry this out because normally they have a wide range of both external and internal contacts; they should be converting those contacts and the information they gain from them.

Training should be for everyone in the organisation at all levels and the role of the top team should be to ensure that training programmes are relevant throughout the organisation, from induction to retirement. An important first step is to ensure that there is an effective induction programme. Induction, like recruitment, is a great opportunity for senior people to become involved with new starters; to paraphrase the Jesuit proverb 'Let me inspire and enthuse an employee during their first six months and I will make them an employee for life'. An important part of the company's induction programme is to introduce the values and the mission of the organisation. If this can be delivered by a member of the top team, it will have far more impetus.

Top managers should pay attention to the way things are done as well as the end result. A greater interest in process on the part of the top management team and more discussion about issues like quality, people development and the development of new systems in the organisation, rather than constant discussions about profit, sales and margins, would encourage people elsewhere in the organisation to think about these issues too. Generally people become interested in the things that they see interest their boss, so people, systems and structures may come some way down the list of their priorities if the boss can only talk about the last set of results and the need 'to get more product out'.

The strategists within the organisation need to ensure that there are the other mechanisms in place which support training and development. Systems like career and succession planning and, more importantly, a clear statement from the company board about their people development policy can be very effective in making people think about issues of performance management and continuous development. Many trainers are concerned that by making the identification of training and development into a more systematic procedure that it becomes yet another mechanical administrative function to be carried out. This, however, has not happened in areas such as budgeting and long range planning, where the department which owns the process has created a structure which focuses individual thinking and some form of pro-forma for managers to work on. It is also important to measure people development and respond quickly to adverse variances.

In several organisations I have found that the budget is normally carried out on time but performance appraisals are sporadic and often only carried out at the last moment (normally about four or five appraisals in a day). The organisation has to ask itself whether the management of people is such a low priority, or is there a lack of direction about the systems which support performance management and management development from the people who own them? The setting of clear and measurable targets is another issue which would highlight the importance of developing people. One of the reasons why little attention is paid to continuous development in some organisations is that it is one of the most difficult areas in which to set measurable standards and targets, and thus it becomes forgotten in an increasingly quantitative world.

Setting targets for the development of people is an important way of ensuring that it stays on the business agenda, and the training and development specialist should be working with top management to identify the standards which are expected of line managers within the organisation in relation to the development and training of their people. Clearly, continuous development of people needs to become something more than a motherhood concept and yet it is still, in many organisations, seen as something that gets a three or four line mention in the annual report and little more.

One of the most critical problems facing organisations is the operation of the *Peter Principle*. The Peter Principle is the title of a well known and amusing book by Lawrence Peter and Raymond Hill (Pan, 1964) which claims that in most organisations people are promoted until they reach a position in which they are incompetent. Sadly, this concept is more than just an amusing subject and is, in fact, a very real problem in many organisations. It is well known in areas like the Health Service, where the best clinician may be promoted to a management position or in sales, where the high-flying sales rep is promoted to sales manager. The organisation may lose a good technician and gain a poor manager. The Peter Principle can be avoided in several ways:

- Technical people can have their own career and salary structures related to technical competence rather than managerial expertise, so

that promoting to a management position is not the only means of increasing status and reward within the organisation.
- People can be prepared well in advance for management positions by training them in the process skills which lead on to management skills, so that when they are promoted to management positions, they are equipped to handle them.
- The organisation can re-emphasise the importance of continuous development so that people take a series of incremental steps rather than a few large steps in their career.

The people at the top of the organisation can ensure that there is a clear policy for equal opportunities within the organisation. We have already seen that glass ceilings prevent full and effective development for women, members of ethnic minorities and the disabled. Organisations need to state unequivocally their commitment to equality of opportunity and work hard to put this commitment into action. This increases the level of competition for the best jobs within the organisation and encourages everyone to strive for them. This healthy competition for key jobs is an important way of increasing personal development. If promotion is automatic, then there is little incentive to learn new skills; if it is the focus of active competition, people are more likely to work hard to learn new skills in order to be well-placed in any selection procedure. This healthy competition, like market forces in the economy, encourages the search for personal growth in order to meet the challenge. A lack of fair competition for top jobs breeds complacency in the 'crown princes' and exasperation in the disenfranchised majority.

Top management within the organisation should participate in the selection of internal training and development advisors. Personnel and training jobs should be seen as important steps in the career development of people with potential. Too often in the past, they have been seen as a resting place for tired executives, although thankfully this has been a diminishing trend in the last few years. Internal professional advisors in areas such as training and development need to be people with not only training competence, but also a high level of managerial competence, and many effective organisations believe that a spell in training and development is an integral part of a career development programme rather than a potentially interesting backwater. The organisation should ensure that only the best people go into this strategically important profession.

Organisations must encourage by whatever means at their disposal, the concept of renewal. The idea that people must refresh and renew their skills to meet the changing needs of their business is relatively new; new to the current generation of workers and managers. Blue-collar workers needing to learn new skills after their old job has been automated; white-collar workers replaced by a computer-based expert system – the people displaced by new technology are still required in our organisations but with a new set of skills. The most important skill we can give to our people at the moment is the ability to ride the waves of change at work by learning to learn, by being able to renew their skills and change their work style so that they can meet the challenge of what is increasingly an unpredictable future.

A STRATEGY FOR TRAINING AND DEVELOPMENT SPECIALISTS

There are three key strategies which training and development specialists must follow in order to ensure that they contribute to greater organisational effectiveness:

1. To move training and development from the periphery of the organisation's activities to the strategic centre.
2. To transfer the day-to-day responsibility for identifying training needs, evaluating and even delivering training to line managers.
3. To raise the levels of training capability generally within the organisation.

The move to the strategic centre

It is important that organisations regard training and development as a central issue in developing their competitive edge. Business strategists increasingly accept that the development of the organisation's capability should be viewed alongside the normal management of business performance. We have already seen that organisations need to introduce capability factors into the performance requirements for their managers and staff; they clearly need to make provision for this in their own business strategies. Training and development is an important aspect of this development of capability. Many trainers, however, seek to stay on the sidelines, rather like timid skaters on an ice rink, because they fear that when they get into the centre they will be knocked over by the seemingly awesome and aggressive people who are in control of the business. They must, however, make strenuous attempts to survive in that strategic centre in order to give the organisation the full benefit of their skills and knowledge. There are number of ways that this can be done:

- They can review the development needs of the whole organisation as well as the training needs of individuals. To do this they need to be fully aware of their organisation's strategy and direction for the future.

- They can run their own departments like a business and create effective mechanisms for the identification of their customer's needs and evaluating how those needs have been met. It is particularly important to manage the whole training cycle, as many trainers feel that their role ends when the top goes back onto the felt tip pen at the end of the training course. Training needs to be followed up at the workplace, handling real issues alongside those managers who have participated in the training programmes to ensure that the main training issues have been fully validated.
- Trainers also need to see themselves as internal consultants and not just as purveyors of individual training courses or training packages. Rather they should be working with managers to think more about broad development solutions to their business problems.

Supporting the Manager as Coach

If most learning takes place in the workplace, it is more important that the line manager acts as trainer and coach rather than leaving this work to the training and development specialists. This process of handing responsibility to line managers needs careful consideration. I would recommend an incremental handover whereby the trainer initially provides a lot of direction on a manager's responsibility for training with the provision of detailed supporting programmes and procedures, but over a period of time releasing responsibility and handing it over in a coherent way so that the manager slowly takes on the coaching role with confidence and the trainer's role begins to change from classroom trainer to supporter and facilitator and ultimately to internal consultant. This is lateral delegation, critically important if the organisation is to ensure that it has the right skills and knowledge to ensure its future survival.

It is usually easier for trainers in the organisation to provide line managers with the skills of self-evaluation rather than help the trainers to understand the detail of every part of the business. Other functions (eg accountancy and marketing) have succeeded in instilling some of their professional disciplines into the general manager within a range of organisations; it is now time for the human resource professional to do the same thing.

Increasing Training Capability

Continuous development of training capability should take place within all organisations in a systematic way, and the concept of trainer capability needs to be examined in a little more detail. We have already seen the need to support line managers as coaches and it is important to increase their understanding of the training/development process. This does not necessarily mean that everyone has to become an accomplished class-room trainer. The main areas of accountability in training are the identification of training needs, the design of training programmes, the delivery of training programmes and the evaluation and validation of training. The identification of training needs and the evaluation of training are areas which should become the domain of the line manager and they will need to understand the relevance of these processes if they are to take a strategic approach to the development of people. Currently training and development planning seems to focus on the selection of a series of packaged solutions from a menu of courses. If we are to fit the solution for development issues more closely to their cause then we need to show managers how to identify training and development needs and how to evaluate the success of the chosen solution. The training and development specialist will play the role of internal consultant, supporting the line manager particularly in the area of selecting an appropriate solution. The design and delivery of programmes is still likely to remain the domain of the professional trainer, although it is likely that the focus will change as programmes become looser in design and more participative in delivery method.

A final point is relevant here on training course design. Trainers often talk about decentralisation and free-flowing organisations and the need to manage change, whilst continuing to design programmes which are highly structured and based around the delivery of management theory. This gives the participants little opportunity to manage change on the programme. There is a great opportunity in the design of training programmes to ensure that they match and model the sort of behaviour that the organisation is trying to encourage. If the organisation is beginning to devolve authority to subsidiary units, then the training course, particularly if it is more than two or three days in length, can actually model the handover of authority in its structure, so that the issues involved in this can be explored on the training programme.

Training programmes are as much about 'real life' as real life itself is. They are a microcosm of business activity and are tremendous opportunities to model and explore real business issues. We can't explore issues of management of change as trainers if we run highly programmed and inflexible courses which offer no possibility of dealing with issues in a way the participants need. Our training and development specialists need to structure courses which are specific and relevant to the needs of the business and the people within it; not packaged programmes of broad and generalised management theory.

There are several things which can be done to ensure that the training programmes are tied closely to the strategy of the business:

- Ensuring that an effective pre-course briefing and post-course follow up is carried out.
- Training courses and workshops should be designed to ensure that an appropriate mix of learning styles is put together with time for activity, reflection and the testing of theory against reality. In particular, it is critical that action planning becomes an integral part of the programme.
- The objectives of the participants should be clarified at an early stage of the training and development event, and there should be a clear learning contract between the trainer and the trainees that those objectives will be met during the workshop due to the efforts of both parties. There needs to be a joint responsibility in setting and achieving learning objectives during a training event. In an organisation which is aiming for high performance, it is unrealistic to maintain the illusion that training is something done *to* an individual *by* someone else. If the training is relevant the individual should know why they are there and should be able to participate actively in the process of achieving their learning objectives.

THE ROLE OF COACH

There are a selection of 'coaching'-type roles which we all may need at times to help us in our development. The first of these roles is that of the professional coach. In many ways, the coaching role is analogous with the role of parent to child. The coach has a direct responsibility for helping our growth and development.

Line managers

The role of the manager as coach has recurred throughout the book. The whole concept of managing performance requires an understanding of the manager's responsibility for managing both the performance and the development of the people working for them.

Our boss normally plays the coaching role in our working life because they have the greatest influence on our development, with an institutionalised responsibility for setting goals, reviewing our performance and giving rewards or reprimands on the basis of that performance. We all need a coach, because most of us lack the complete objectivity to review and manage our own performance. A good coach is both committed to and detached from our performance – someone who is on our side, someone who wants us to win but who at the same time is sufficiently detached and objective to give us feedback in the way that helps us to improve our performance. A good coach needs to be a 'good enough manager' which is the managerial equivalent of the psychologist's concept of the 'good enough mother'. The good enough mother is not perfect, not omnipresent but is there when needed and provides sufficient support for the child to enable them to grow and develop. The good enough mother is contrasted with both the 'absentee mother' who provides no support for the child and the 'perfect mother' who smothers the child with love and affection, taking them over, giving them restrictive boundaries and no scope to grow as an individual.

Likewise, the good enough manager is neither too hard, leaving their staff exposed without support or guidance; nor too soft, cushioning them from harsh reality and 'nannying' them through the working day. This concept is at the heart of effective coaching, managing people by challenge and stimulation whilst providing the necessary support and guidance. It is a difficult act to balance but a critical one.

Peer coaching

Coaching is not just a boss:subordinate issue, there are other people from whom we may gain support and to whom we may offer it. Peer coaching, analogous to our siblings when we were children, can give us feedback and advice in a less threatening way than our boss. When we want to discuss something in a more speculative way, we may find it more convenient and less formal to discuss with a well meaning colleague than to take it up in a more formal way with our boss.

One of the most telling signs of effective teamwork is when colleagues are able to get behind the façades of formality and politeness to give each other frank and unvarnished feedback. This is a positive benefit to all parties and creates an alternative source of feedback and advice to the line manager.

Many people have found that a more formal 'learning partnership' in which a group of two to five people meet to work together and discuss work-based issues to learn from each other is helpful. A more formalised version of this has been set up by Ashridge Management College in their Action Learning Sets for Managing Directors, in which managing directors from various organisations sit down together to discuss issues and learn from each other, normally with a skilled facilitator available to give structure and perspective to the discussions.

Mentor

Mentoring has grown in popularity as an alternative to coaching. The mentor is seen as someone who gives general guidance from a different perspective than one's line manager – often at a more senior level or perhaps from another function. To complete my family analogy, the mentor may be a grandparent figure, available to discuss longer term issues, particularly in areas such as career development and influencing skills.

Often the mentor is used for high flier programmes or positive action/ equal opportunity programmes where, for example, women in a senior role act as mentors to younger women who may be experiencing difficulties in breaking through some of those glass ceilings I referred to earlier.

Mentoring may be formal or informal but can be a particularly effective means of giving people support in an organisation alternative to the normal line management coaching process.

SELF DEVELOPMENT

Effective performance management involves the interaction between the organisation and the individual. This interaction is regulated by the intervention of the manager – the main management role is to oversee the performance cycle and to contribute to the development of the individual.

The most important outcome of this role is the emergence of people within the organisation who are capable of managing their own performance and development. The more people who can do this, the more managers can work on other issues which relate to the strategic development of the organisation. In fact, this empowering of people within the organisation is a necessary precondition of new strategic development – change has to be preceded by the capability to put the change into effect. The organisation of the future with its adhocracies and its flexible structures will need to be staffed by people who are self-managing.

The key to this is to encourage people to see themselves as their own boss – literally as freelances who happen to be with a particular organisation at a particular time. With that change in perception people can completely transform their approach to personal development. It creates an immediate move from wage slave to an independent professional with a set of skills and knowledge to use as they wish. With this approach, everyone can complement the programme of performance contracts by approaching them as an equal partner with rights and obligations, not as humble employee who has been pressurised into working for the organisation.

This paradigm shift from employee to contractor is important both for the individual and for the organisation. The organisation benefits because it has a whole new group of people thinking about their contribution to the organisation rather than waiting for instructions. However, by raising levels of initiative within the organisation, the top management team must increase its own ability to manage diversity and ambiguity. Directors are facing the same dilemma which has been faced by parents of adolescents for generations – how much authority to give and how far can we tolerate things being done differently to our own cherished methods which have stood us so well in the past.

The issue is no longer whether it can be done, but whether we can afford not to increase the initiative of our people. The world is changing so rapidly that we have to encourage decision-making at the lowest possible level in order to increase the numbers of people who are 'sensing' the environment and making decisions about what needs to be done. Empowering people in this way is no longer just a nice thing to do, it has become an essential thing to do. We all know that we can choose our friends but we are stuck with our family and our boss. If our boss doesn't manage our development well, this must not condemn us to a lifetime of low achievement. We have to set our own targets and manage our own development. It is immensely helpful, however, for people who want to manage themselves to have a good boss around somewhere to act as a safety net and coach, when they have problems.

One of the most important mechanisms for carrying out a review of your own development is to use the well tried marketing technique of the SWOT analysis. This is as relevant for the individual as it is for the organisation because the individual, in order to develop effectively, has to have a clear idea about their strengths and weaknesses in relation to the needs of their working environment. The SWOT analysis encourages development in a direction that is relevant to the overall direction of their company. One of the most well-known pieces of advice given in career planning is – find out what you are good at and get somebody to pay you to do it. That is still relevant and important as it implies that what you are good at has to be a marketable skill and has to be important to the organisation in which you work.

Let us examine each of the four parts of the SWOT analysis – strengths, weaknesses, opportunities and threats.

Strengths It is always important to know where we perform well. It is normally from our strengths that our genuine achievements arise. As a personnel manager my first question in career counselling discussions has always been – what do you do well? Our career progression does not consist of minimising our weaknesses; it consists of maximising our strengths.

Weaknesses We need to address the question of weaknesses or limitations – those things that prevent us from performing as effectively as we might – and what we need to do to resolve them. If necessary, refer again to Chapter Ten which reviews the series of gaps and barriers which prevent people from performing within an organisation.

Opportunities and Threats Essentially this is an analysis of trends which are taking place within the organisation and possibly within the wider context of the economy and society. What things are going on that will enable us to capitalise on our strengths and remove our weaknesses? Opportunities are those trends which are moving in our direction and threats are those trends which may prevent us ultimately from achieving the levels of performance that we wish to attain. It is more exhilarating (and less exhausting) to ride the waves of change to our destination rather than to swim against them. Our first step is to identify those trends. One of the key factors in self development is to be fully aware of what is going on in the wider context and not just purely on the job that we are doing today and will need to do tomorrow. This involves reading widely, talking to people about how they see the future and ensuring that we are fully briefed on the range of social trends, what John Naisbitt and Patricia Aburdene describe in *Megatrends* (Futura, 1982). Doctors in the National Health Service who have concentrated on treating patients and tried to ignore the major political and social changes taking place in the Health Service; head teachers who have preferred to concentrate on running the academic parts of their school and ignored the increasing trend to local management of schools within the education service, managers of products who concentrate on meeting their targets and are so focused on the achievement of today's target that they fail to look beyond into the way the world is changing. All these people will find life very difficult in the future and will be a considerable step behind the winners. Tunnel vision is one of the worst problems for managers and the effective self developer must be observing and sensing the environment regularly to ensure that they are aware of current and future trends.

The SWOT analysis is a technique borrowed from the marketing function and in order to develop effectively we need to market ourselves. The SWOT analysis is the first and most important part of this process; to clarify where we are in relation to our business environment and to generate our priorities for future development. We also need to think of some of the tactics of marketing ourselves and to leverage the power and authority that we have.

The first priority is self-promotion. This should not be confused with self-aggrandisement – you should not just be telling people how good you are! We promote ourselves by being *visible* within our organisation. It is not sufficient to be competent, it is also necessary to be seen to be so; speaking, lecturing or possibly by writing reports or papers. It is, however, important to be aware that we can only promote ourselves effectively after we have built up a track record of competence and performance. When we market ourselves, that also involves more than just telling people how good we are; it involves a process of developing a good track record of effective performance and making sure that people are aware of that. If people are aware of our competence we are more likely to be given the opportunities to grow and develop. There are many people tucked away in corners of organisations who are doing a first rate job but who feel aggrieved at their lack of visibility. This is often because of their failure to promote themselves or to be influential with people in the organisation.

Career planning is becoming increasingly difficult in the modern age. At one time people had a very clear idea of the career path that they should take and this was analogous to climbing up a staircase, moving up a particular career path one step at a time. This is no longer the case; as the staircases have fewer and fewer steps but with much larger gaps between them, career development has become more a matter of expansion rather than promotion. We expand our competence, we expand our levels of expertise and we expand our perspective from a narrow functional view to a broad overview of the needs of the business. At one time it was regarded as important to have a specialised knowledge of a particular subject and to deepen that knowledge until you became head of a function. Nowadays we tend to regard a specialism as an important base for development rather than as an end in itself. It is still important to become very competent, at an early stage in our career at one particular thing, but people who develop effectively use that as a base to develop other skills, so that their perspective does not remain narrow and functional and so that they can make good commercial use of those specialised skills.

The key to the concept of renewal is the idea of continuous personal development. This will only be achieved when organisations create the climate, training specialists provide the skills, managers begin to work effectively as coaches and people accept responsibility for developing themselves in the most effective way possible so that they can cope in whatever economic climate develops.

A further support to the concept of continuous development is the clarification of competence. As we saw earlier, competence analysis – both in terms of job competence and generic competency – can be of great help in defining the characteristics of successful people within the organisation, particularly if those competences are analysed in relation to the organisation's critical success factors. A clear set of competences can help in the following ways:

- They enable top management to state clearly the sort of behaviour which will make the organisation's mission achievable.
- They enable managers to assess people against a common set of agreed criteria.
- They enable the organisation to take a regular stocktake of the capability of their people.
- If clearly stated and widely published, they give individuals an unambiguous guide to their own personal development targets.
- They facilitate movement across functions by setting out clearly which skills are generic and, therefore, transferable.
- They make 'competence gaps' easier to define and, therefore, easier to resolve.

13

Restructuring for Performance

The way an organisation structures itself is a critical factor in the management of individual and organisational performance. However competent an individual may be, they will always be constrained by the organisation structure in which they operate. A 'good' organisation structure cannot guarantee high performance but a bad structure can almost guarantee poor performance. In some of the recent studies of performance management the question of organisation structure has received little attention. My aim is not to create a definitive model of organisational structure but to point to some of the important issues which organisations need to address if they are to take away some of their restrictive barriers that prevent employees from achieving both continuous improvement both of the business and themselves.

There are several themes covered in this chapter that require some explanation.

Simplifying

The first theme is the critical importance of simplifying, particularly important in the management of large organisations. Working in the modern organisation gives one a huge sense of its complexity, which increases as more business strategists acknowledge the importance of segmentation of the marketplace within most industries. This complexity causes much confusion for employees about the process of getting things done and I have often had the feeling, both as a manager, consultant and consumer, that I have needed a competent guide to lead me through the systems and procedures which underpin most modern organisations.

The complexity of organisations would be tolerable if it were not to the detriment of the people struggling to achieve things within this great leviathan. The effect is to drain the energy of employees who spend more time working out how to get things done through 'the system' than actually improving and developing the business. How many of us have stalled on a terrific business idea because it has been just too difficult to manoeuvre it through the myriad levels of management and the network of co-ordinating committees? We need to 'declutter' our organisations so that people concentrate on the important issues instead of wasting time on maintenance activities.

Structure follows strategy

Our organisation's structure depends very much on the business strategy which we wish to adopt. Focusing on a particular niche requires specialisation, responsiveness and devolution of authority to the people who have the greatest understanding of the needs of that market segment. A broad cost strategy may require a greater element of centralisation to ensure economies of scale and the delivery of consistent standards across the whole organisation. Different strategies require different structures to enable them to be delivered.

Without a clear idea of strategy, the organisation structure becomes meaningless. Structure will only be fully effective if it supports the organisational strategy. I understand that osteopaths and chiropractors believe that 'function follows structure'. By this they mean that the body can only function within the constraints of its physiological structure and that structural problems reduce functional effectiveness. This is entirely true of organisations – their structure is the element which helps to convert strategy and policy into activity. If the structure is unwieldy then it will not move into action as quickly; conversely, a good structure is ineffective if it is not underpinned by an agreed strategy.

The critical issues for a business organisation are *'What are we trying to achieve?'* and *'How do we need to be organised in order to achieve our goals consistently?'*

Harnessing energy

Organisations are full of energy. People moving, thinking, doing and creating. No organisation can crush that huge tide of individual energy – even in concentration camps and prisoner of war camps, people set up schools and escape committees, organised games and created works of art. That energy is manifested in the drive of people to *do* something, to make their mark in life and to differentiate themselves from others. I have often been struck by the tendency of people in relatively unskilled jobs to create a life for themselves outside work and devote themselves to creative and imaginative hobbies. If only some of that energy could be channelled into achieving the organisation's business goals.

Energy can either be concentrated or dissipated; the choice is often resultant on the structure of the organisation. A bad structure can crush initiative or, more likely, channel it in the wrong direction. A good structure will encourage initiative and creativity, giving it room to grow whilst ensuring that it is channelled towards the objectives of the business. Management consultants talk about tight and loose properties of organisations. If an organisation is too 'tight' then initiative and energy will be suppressed. If an organisation is too 'loose' then energy is dissipated because it may not be focused on achieving the organisation's objectives. A good structure steers and directs as well as encourages initiative and stimulates energy. This is a key role of the performance contract process.

Restructure, don't tinker

Clarify the organisation structure you need for the future, communicate it to people in a way that respects their fears and concerns, move to it and stay with it. Organise for the future so that you can cope with any major change and keep that structure fundamentally the same – you may add new products or projects but arrange your structure so that they can be assimilated as easily as possible.

If devising an effective structure is good for performance, constant tinkering and organisational reviewing is bad for performance. It creates a feeling of uncertainty and, again, dissipates energy into internal politics, jostling for position and anxiety about future prospects – energy that should be directed towards improving the business. Restructuring for performance is critical but constant minor reorganisations create more problems and detract from effective personal performance.

Subsidiarity

There is another key principle in structuring the organisation: that of subsidiarity. I have already referred to E F Schumacher in *Small is Beautiful* who quoted the papal encyclical *Quadragesima Anno* as follows:

> It is an injustice and at the same time a grave evil and disturbance of right order to assign to a greater and higher association what lesser and subordinate organisations can do.

In real terms, this means that organisations should delegate authority to the lowest level possible provided that the subordinate is appropriate and capable of handling the authority. This should be supported by a lean organisation structure so that there is no danger of that authority being taken away again by more senior people with little to do.

Subsidiarity is not a formula for compulsive devolution; it is an important organising principle which brings accountability and authority down to a level where it can be used most effectively. The Catholic Church, which operates with only a few layers, has effectively managed a world-wide church during the last two millennia by delegating authority to the man on the spot who has been imbued with a very clear sense of organisational mission.

No one best way

Before looking in more detail at organisation structures, it goes without saying that there isn't any one best structure. There are so many factors which have an impact on the organisation's structure – market, geography, products, services, technology and nature of the work – that to prescribe a particular type of structure is unhelpful and inappropriate. The work of defining the right organisation structure can be a lengthy process – it involves a detailed analysis of strategy, customer base and long-term objectives.

Thinking about structure is, however, one of the most important jobs which a top team can do. The effectiveness of an organisation creates a boundary for the performance of the organisation, and to ensure that work flows in the direction of the organisation's strategy is one of the prime activities for people at the top; it must be their responsibility to identify and prevent organisational blockages and to unclutter the organisation so that people are given the scope to perform well but within the set boundaries.

THE GOOD AND BAD ORGANISATION

Before looking at some of features of effective organisation structures I want to cover the effects of good and bad organisational structures by writing some pen pictures of effective and ineffective structures at various levels within different types of business. These are presented in the case study on the following page.

The impact of the two management styles is that while the grocery department is an orderly and civilised place to work, the fresh food department is alive with frenetic activity. The fresh food manager's style is highly directive, issuing a constant stream of instructions from opening to closing time. The grocery manager seems more relaxed and is seen much more by the store manager and by customers – often, like a good head waiter, checking that things are satisfactory and passing the time of day with them. The supervisors thrive under this relaxed leadership and feel a pride in their area of operation. They are completely accountable for

Case study: Team level

There are two main departments in a small independent supermarket; the grocery department which deals with tinned and packaged dry grocery and a frozen foods cabinet and the fresh food department which has a meat, produce and delicatessen section as well as a small in-store bakery.

The grocery manager has four supervisors, each of whom have responsibility for one part of the department. Their role is to ensure that the shelves are fully stocked and they should be available to answer any queries from customers. Every day, there is a brief team meeting in order to discuss delivery schedules, any change in stocking plan and to familiarise each other with their work schedules to ensure that they all understand each other's work in case of absence. There is a clear understanding of the decisions they can make individually and which decisions need to be referred to the grocery manager. Generally, there are a set of agreed procedures on stock rotation, stock levels and ordering; they each understand how to deal with customers complaints and how they should respond in terms of returning or replacing unsatisfactory goods.

Contrast this with the fresh food department. The fresh food manager prefers to keep a tight grip on the department. He has a supervisor for each part of the department, although that supervisor is normally required to check with the manager before laying out stock or ordering new products; in fact, the fresh food manager normally insists on ordering all stock himself in order to keep an eye on costs. All customer complaints must be referred upwards, so that the manager can deal with customers – he prefers to judge each complaint on its merits and so indulges in a lengthy discussion about each complaint to ascertain when the product was bought, its condition, how it was cooked and so on.

their part of the store and thus work hard to ensure that it is kept clean and well-stocked. They talk things over with their boss and introduce new ideas in consultation with him.

The fresh food supervisors feel harassed and unrecognised. Their boss has little time to spare to talk to them and tends to take work off them if it is not done to his satisfaction. He loses staff frequently, due, in his view, to their inability to handle hard work. He believes staff turnover is lower in grocery because of the easy life that they all seem to have over there.

The moral: managing a team is about setting clear responsibilities and supporting people to get on with them. Five people who can understand their job and get on with it will always get more done than one person who is over-burdened and over-stretched with a team who receive work assignments on an ad-hoc basis. People also need to understand the whole picture so that their work integrates thoroughly with the work of their colleagues.

Case study: Unit level

There are two infant schools in a large country town. Both are of a similar size and with roughly the same sort of catchment area. They both cater for children from 4 to 7 years old and thus were both involved in the introduction of the assessment tests in support of the National Curriculum aimed, during the first year of assessment, at seven year olds.

The first school, West Road Primary, asked for the test information at an early stage and made a plan to allocate areas of responsibility to each teacher, regardless of their class responsibility or year group. One teacher was responsible for studying the English curriculum, one for studying the Maths curriculum, another for the Science curriculum tests and so on. They were each charged with making a short presentation at a staff meeting four weeks later regarding their proposals for managing the assessment process within their area of operation. This meeting took place, all staff were briefed and an action plan drawn up for the teachers of the seven year olds' class to carry out the assessment tests with appropriate support from other teachers, namely watching over seven year old pupils while they were *not* undergoing their assessments and also providing invaluable advice and support in terms of their own area of expertise that they had researched so thoroughly in the weeks prior to the assessment.

The second school, East Road Primary, distributed all the curriculum papers to all staff in order to encourage their involvement in the whole process. They asked for comments on the pack of papers so that these could be passed on to the Year Two teachers (those teachers responsible for organising the assessment tests for seven year olds) to enable them to plan their programme of testing whilst ensuring that the rest of their class of seven year olds were occupied while they were assessing small groups of four or five.

The experience of the two schools was quite different for the same event. West Road found the following:

- Breaking the work up created a feeling of challenge and accountability for each person but not so great that they felt overwhelmed by it.
- They managed the change effectively and with the equal involvement of everyone.
- They created an ad hoc organisation structure based on functional expertise, overlaying their normal class responsibility.
- They resolved a short-term need but in doing so also created a new group of subject specialists who would be able to build on that knowledge in the future.
- By involving everyone in reviewing the individual work, they created a team not only with specialised knowledge (and thus an individual contribution) but also with an understanding of where their specialism fitted into the broader picture. This increased team cohesion by increasing the school's capacity to provide mutual support and guidance.
- The two teachers who carried out the assessments felt confident in the support of their colleagues.

East Road found the following:

- Trying to give everyone a broad understanding of everything created the lowest common denominator of understanding. The job was so big that *a*) no-one felt inclined to really get into it and *b*) there was no sense of individual accountability for the task.
- No-one increased their understanding of any subject, they were merely confirmed in their view that the assessment tests put an unfair burden on teachers and were a 'bad thing'.
- The two teachers who carried out the tests felt alone and unsupported. The others viewed the next year, when they may be one of the two teachers involved, with dread.
- Instead of an opportunity for the team to pull together in a common cause, the team was pushed further apart.
- Levels of stress in the school were high and this was transmitted to the children. Parents complained about the rushed nature of the assessment programme.

Incidentally, at West Road school four days after the tests were completed, a parent rang the school to ask them when the assessments would begin. She was surprised to hear that they had already been completed.

Case study: Organisational level

Two finance Houses competed in similar sectors – motor finance, personal finance and office equipment finance. They both had offices throughout Great Britain.

The first one, Finance Incorporated, carried out a reorganisation on a geographic basis. It set up business centres across the country with generalist teams of sales people who were able to provide cover across all business areas. They reported into a sales director based in London, who was part of a board of directors which included a new business development director and a marketing director.

The second, Consolidated Financial Holdings, organised itself on a business centre basis with a director for each business area responsible for sales, marketing and new business development within their own market. They set up regional centres for each operation but with specialist sales teams working in each sector.

The results of the two re-organisations were as shown in Table 6:

Table 6 *Good v bad organisational structures*

Consolidated Financial Holdings	Finance Incorporated
• Developed a closer understanding of each of their business areas.	• Developed a closer understanding of their regional areas. Unfortunately with increasing investment in new technology, physical proximity was no longer an important factor in the buying decision in any of the sectors.
• Was able to make a quick response to changing circumstances in each of their business sectors. The relevant business director had a high level of authority to make changes in the business, particularly in relation to interest rates, without having to refer to colleagues.	• Needed to gain approval from sales, new business and marketing directors to any major operational change – this was rarely forthcoming because of the possible consequences in other parts of the business and the low adaptability of the sales force to any changes.

- Developed a more specialised team and a closer relationship with customers because of their greater understanding of the business. Regular communication meetings with their colleagues in the other sectors enabled them to keep in touch with each other's business.
- New business and sales departments, as part of the same team, could introduce and test new business ideas quickly, acting responsively on the results of pilot programmes.

- Found it more difficult to spread their knowledge across three sectors and found little compensation in understanding the local business environment. More regular training needed because of the need to keep up to date over such a wide area of activity.
- The new business development team had difficulty in working with and influencing the sales force because they worked in separate functional silos – sending ideas up to the new business director, who in turn spoke to the sales director who ultimately introduced the idea to the sales team.

These are all real examples which I have experienced personally (with the names and the industries changed to protect me from the lawyers!). There are many more examples of situations where a change in structure has led to further changes in individual performance and business performance. Good structures bring the organisation closer to their market; they facilitate fast and effective decision making; they direct people's energy towards developing new business or improving business performance and give people an identifiable unit to which they can respond as well as developing pride in their work.

Bad structures create unnecessary maintenance work; they blur accountabilities and make people feel frustrated and bitter in the knowledge that they could do so much, if only the structure would allow them.

Now we look at how the organisation can begin to restructure to create a high performance environment. There are two basic tasks – simplifying and clarifying.

SIMPLIFYING

The time has come for organisations to clear their decks, so that only the important things get done. Like tidying up the office or clearing out the attic, it involves creating space to retain in good order the things you want to retain, rather than clutter your living space with things that you think you may need. It involves concentration on the essentials at the expense of the peripherals.

Delayering

The most important process of simplification that an organisation can go through is the reduction of levels of management and, by extension, increasing spans of control. Traditionally, large organisations have carried several layers of management and have developed into the 'Russian doll' type of organisation – a series of gradually smaller jobs fitting inside each other. Excessive layers of management make each job more difficult to do by creating longer lines of communication. Even worse than this logistical problem is that each of those levels feels the need to reconstitute the job in hand and reinterpret the objectives as they are passed down. This creates confusion and a drift away from the organisation's original mission.

Carrying out a delayering exercise has several implications. First, there is an immediate change in perspective from promotion to development. In a heavily layered organisation, career planning is more a question of planning promotions and jumps from grade to grade, rather than a continuous process of development. With fewer levels of management, there are less step changes and thus development becomes continuous and incremental, driven by the capability requirements of the business rather than by the company's promotion system.

Secondly, fewer levels of management increases the concentration of authority and therefore of accountability. There are less people in the hierarchy each taking their own little bit of authority and so it becomes concentrated rather than diffuse.

A delayered organisation also gives people more room to grow. In an organisation with several management layers, people very quickly bump up against their next level of management. There is a natural, and probably quite unconscious, tendency for the higher level to keep their subordinates at a lower level of development and initiative in order to protect their own authority. In organisations like NUCOR in the United States, where foremen have a wide range of accountability, very large spans of control, and report into a unit manager, they have almost unlimited opportunities to grow and develop their teams. The boundaries are much wider and their accountabilities much greater than in an environment where they are immediately constrained by a hierarchy of plant and works management.

As a result, the tendency in a delayered organisation, because of the wide boundaries (particularly vertically), is for far fewer 'turf fights'. In a minimalist organisation, (ie an organisation which is staffed at minimum levels) there is far less possible overlap and thus fewer demarcation disputes.

An organisation should always be as lean as possible. It encourages people to think more creatively about how jobs should be done with less resources, as well as concentrating the mind on value added tasks rather than on maintenance activity, on output rather than input. However, whilst saying that removing levels of management may be an important feature of effective performance, this should be carried out so that the commitment of the middle managers and the organisation as a whole is retained. We are approaching the mid-life crisis of the middle manager and, as in any period of crisis, it is important that it should be handled sensitively. Currently many organisations are going through massive restructuring, which is normally focused on the middle manager's role. This is quite natural – there will always be a need for strategic direction within an organisation; there will also always be a need for first line management in order to provide direction and support to the people who are actually doing the job. It is always likely to be the management levels in the middle of the organisation who find it most difficult to justify their existence and who become trapped between the strategy developers and the implementers. The front line manager, responsible for coaching and developing a team of people, can find immense satisfaction in that role. The directors too, at the top of the organisation, will normally find their responsibility for developing strategy and setting the future direction of the organisation to be a challenging and stimulating job. However, sandwiched in the middle of a large organisation is the tranche of middle managers desperately trying to define their position and to give their role justification. These middle managers are normally men and women who have been successful as first line managers and are waiting in an ever-lengthening queue for directorships and other top management roles. While waiting they become 'post boxes'; another stage of management to be 'got through', hovering over their subordinates, preventing them from maximising their potential and frustrating the plans of top management through inertia. All of this, of course, is subconscious and not deliberate. These people finally rush to accept early retirement at 50 and retire frustrated and embittered, whilst one of their more talented subordinates is promoted into their place and the cycle begins again.

These middle managers, however, are normally people with valuable experience, skill and knowledge. They are promoted from their first line role precisely because of that experience and also because of their energy and effectiveness as front line managers. The frustrating element of this cycle is that those people are promoted out of an area in which they are very effective and into a job for which they have very little training and even less understanding. Delayering needs to be done carefully, so that it removes the barriers to effectiveness within the organisation, whilst still retaining the commitment and goodwill of middle managers within it. This can be done in several ways.

Organisations must review and reconceive the role of the middle manager They are a group of people with ability and relevant experience crying out to be used to their full potential. Their role needs to be defined as they have an important contribution to make as specialist advisers to the people who work for them and to the people who develop the strategy in the organisation. Middle managers often occupy that valuable middle ground where strategy is converted into activity – the area of tactical implementation. They are normally experienced enough to know the line management job, and far-sighted enough to understand how it fits in with strategy. If they are not, they should be removed in any case. Those who are should be encouraged to use that experience more effectively.

Organisations should delayer in the most sensitive way wherever possible One way of paving the way for this is to change the nature of the job evaluation scheme into fewer broad grades, rather than a large number of narrow grades. Managers are also more likely to find delayering more acceptable if they see it as a general organisational restructuring and not implying ineffectiveness on their part. These people are *not* inefficient and incompetent; the organisation restructures because it doesn't need the variety of levels in the organisation that it has required before. Therefore, the delayering process should be carried out as sensitively as possible and supported by extensive redeployment and retraining programmes.

The important issue of communication Organisations are not delayering primarily in order to save money – although this may be an important by-product – they are doing it in order to create a culture in which people are given more room to perform and grow. It is important, therefore, that they make very clear the reasons for their restructuring exercise, and use the opportunity to explain to other people in the organisation the importance of focusing clearly on strategic objectives and on creating an environment where people can work.

Finally, reducing layers of management will only work if those remaining layers are competent managers with high quality management development and training. A smaller cadre of high quality managers will prove more effective and responsive than a larger group with an ill-defined role.

Sub-contracting

One of the trends which complicates organisational life has been the growth in professional specialists. These are people who have often brought well-honed professional skills into the organisation, but in some cases have also created systems and procedures which have over-complicated the way that organisations operate. One way of making these specialists more effective may be to create a structure which, instead of linking them into a functional hierarchy, moves them out into the line, to provide professional support for a general manager in charge of a product or service. This would create an organisation which is broad rather than tall, and would have the effect of directing the work of the specialist into broader business objectives.

Alternatively, the work of specialists could be subcontracted out to other organisations and consultants. The process of sub-contracting is one which has been dealt with at some length by Charles Handy in several of his books – particularly *The Future of Work* (Blackwell, 1984), and *The Age of Unreason*. He has forecast a future where organisations are made up of a core of highly committed people, supported by a contractual fringe, paid in fees not wages, and on results, not time. The contractual fringe would work very much as it works now in both construction and advertising. These specialists would not be required by the organisation all the time, but their skills could be brought in from time to time to work on a particular project or to resolve a particular problem.

The contractual fringe is particularly relevant to performance management because there are several implications for the overall effectiveness of the business.

Concentration on core business by permanent staff

Subcontracting several specialisms within the organisation enables the core of the organisation to concentrate on the achievement of the organisation's mission; those parts of the business that it knows and does well. The business will never be able to subcontract all the 'non-core' work to other people because they will still need broadly-based, functional specialists in the main support areas – finance, personnel, marketing etc., some of whom are keys to understanding the values and mission of the organisation and could not possibly carry out their work if they operated as sub-contractors. The three that I have named are integral to the smooth working of the operation, and their complete absence would leave line managers vulnerable in some of the critical parts of their business. The key functional professionals would have an important role in relation to the sub-contractors. They would become skilled in translating the needs of the business into the appropriate functional language and acting as intermediaries, so that the work of the sub-contractor was both functionally sound and directly relevant to the business. This happens now in marketing; many organisations have marketing directors who are able to brief and evaluate the work of a range of subcontractors – market research agencies, advertising agencies and so on, and direct their specialised skills into useful projects.

Unbiased opinions

Subcontracting gives organisations access to a very wide range of expert opinion. It means that they can consult experts in particularly specialised areas, who are well up-to-date with new methods and approaches in their area of specialised knowledge. Sub-contracting gives access to specialists without drawing them into the structure of the organisation.

Fixed term contracts

Using outside specialists as 'sub contractors' supports the organisational aim of decluttering. These external specialists do their job and go. Internal specialists do their job and stay, even when there are workload troughs when their work may not be required to the same extent. An important part of working with external specialists should be the handing over of the work back to line managers. Often this is not the case with internal specialists who set something up and continue to run it in perpetuity, often in order to meet their own objectives rather than those of the business.

Minimising fixed overheads

The most important economic implication of using subcontractors is the nature of their cost. Organisations are normally looking to transfer as many costs as possible from fixed to variable. A short analysis of the cost of an employee, particularly a management employee in a specialist function, demonstrates the high cost of labour. The formula normally goes something like salary + pension + on-costs + secretarial assistance + office/car parking space + departmental costs. The use of external specialists who normally arrange their own pension, buy their own car, work from an office at home or in a small business centre and do their own administration reduces the need for organisations to buy in these additional support facilities.

The sub-contracting process is an important initiative in reducing the amount of work done within the organisation. It simplifies organisations whilst giving access to a wide range of expertise. This expertise gives an organisation access to genuinely specialised support without creating an excessively complicated organisation.

CLARIFICATION

Having simplified the organisation, with the right numbers of people working towards the corporate mission, the next critical task for the organisation is to clarify what it wants people to achieve in their role and how it wants people to operate.

Many current management writers have emphasised the need to manage in chaos. I believe that a simple structure and a clear method of operation with an understanding of how to get things done in the organisation are very important ways of managing within that disorder.

In order to create the right sort of structure in which people can flourish, organisations need to clarify the following:

- The basis of their structure.
- What levels of work need to be carried out.
- Reporting lines.
- How decisions should be made and implemented.
- Individual accountability and authority.

The basis of their structure

Several factors determine the sort of structure that an organisation requires; significantly, many of these determinants have themselves undergone significant change in the last few years.

Size is one of the most important variables. At both extremes, very small organisations need a relatively light organisation structure and there is a need for greater formality as the organisation grows bigger and more complex.

The technology of an organisation also has significant implications. Effective technology in both the operation and the infrastructure can extend spans of control by reducing the need for detailed supervision.

Geographical location can have a profound effect on the effectiveness of an organisation structure. An organisation whose units are geographically disparate may generate different structures and mechanisms for coordination from one which has its main operating unit based in one area. Information technology is, however, minimising the problems of geographical dispersion. Events can be controlled from a distance and even, with video and satellite television technology, form effective communication networks.

Different markets require different types of organisation structures. A niche market requires small, flexible and responsive organisational units with decision making placed at a much lower level in the parent organisation to support that. A mass or highly standardised market needs an organisation structure with the 'brain' at Head Office, but with very strong systems to drive centrally agreed decisions down to operating units as quickly and effectively as possible. This is particularly true of large hotel and retail chains where there is increasing pressure to produce a service of consistently high quality.

The people in the organisation have an important impact on the way the organisation is structured. Their aspirations, work style and career progression has very much to be taken into account within the organisation. Professional organisations like accountancy practices tend to have very little day-to-day organisation structure; rather a series of groupings of professionals who work in a particular style. If the people within the organisation are largely autonomous then spans of control immediately increase. This is an effective feature of performance management because of the scope that it provides for individual growth, which is, in many professional organisations, one of their main attractions for high calibre professional staff.

Work flow should not be overlooked when setting up an organisation structure. However it is important to ensure that it does not entirely dictate the structure of the whole organisation. Functional structures, where people of a similar type need to work closely together, have been a feature of organisational life – the classic 'silo' approach, where work flows up and down a function and only rarely flows across. There may be synergy benefits to grouping people of similar professional competence together but equally there may be disadvantages in excessive concentrating of specialists – the so-called ghetto effect.

There are many deeper issues to take into account when designing the structure of the organisation. However this is not the place for a detailed analysis of structural issues. From this brief review of the determinants of structure it seems that there are two sets of forces which act on an organisation in its search for structure. One set is outward looking – organising around the market or client; the other set is introspective – organising around the work of the organisation and the needs of the people within it. This balance between external and internal perspectives is critical in relation to structure. The need to look both outwards and inwards at the same time is equally important and is all part of the dualism of the modern business organisation. The two views create a number of benefits (see Table 7).

Table 7 *Benefits of external and internal focus*

External focus	*Internal focus*
• Responsiveness	• Efficiency of operation
• Understanding of customer needs	• Understanding of employee needs
• General product understanding	• 'Centres of Excellence' for functions
• Coordination of the end product	• Coordination of the process
• Revenue enhancement	• Cost control
• Product excellence	• Functional excellence

The priority within the business needs may dictate where the structure should be on a continuum between two extremes.

Bureaucracies based on a drive towards efficiency often fail to respond rapidly to customer needs and thus are inappropriate in a rapidly shifting marketplace. Devolved or decentralised structures are responsive to changing circumstances but need to be tolerant of some inefficiences and allow a variety of approaches to the organisation's business. The matrix structure is a balance of both – the lower risk option. The matrix structure should not always be seen as the perfect solution; it may be too rigid in some situations and too complex in others.

There is no best structure – no one structure contains every element of rightness in it. There are only appropriate structures which help the organisation achieve its business strategy and inappropriate structures which hinder that achievement.

Before moving on, we can summarise the components of an effective organisation structure:

- The organisation needs a strategic group – reviewing and sensing the environment and translating external needs into internal strategies. This is the *direction* function.
- The structure needs a function which translates strategies into action plans for people within the organisation and monitors their achievement. This is the *management* function.
- There should be a way of organising and monitoring the work of front line people – this is the *supervising* function.
- Normally, people need to actually do the work of the organisation within the constraints of policy and plans set by the other functions.
- Most organisations need access to specialised support in areas such as marketing, law, information technology, personnel and training. This support may be inside or outside the organisation but still needs to be available.

- Mechanisms are needed to coordinate the work of different sections and functions within the organisation to ensure that it is all directed towards similar or complementary objectives.
- The structure must create a sense of belonging to either a work group, unit or division. There is a need to identify with a group of colleagues – the hunting band in Anthony Jay's famous *Corporation Man* (Cape, 1972) analogy – and also a larger entity; the tribe. This, of course, is the essence of the British Army's enthusiasm for the regiment – a unit with character and tradition to which the individual soldier can relate. This identification makes people *want* to achieve the organisational goals both for themselves, their colleagues and their unit.

These components need to be present in every part of every organisation. Even a football club needs a leadership function, a control mechanism, access to specialised support (groundsmen etc), coordination of individual effort and a feeling of identity which creates and sustains the desire to achieve both one's own goals and the goals of the organisation.

The next issue is how these components will be allocated.

Clarity of function

The different activities do not need to be carried out by different people. In a small organisation, the function of developing and managing strategy may be carried out by one person, who may buy in specialist support. In a large organisation several people may carry out functions such as management, although one must ask carefully what value each level adds to the organisation. An organisation with several levels between strategy and implementation needs to establish clearly the responsibilities at each level, otherwise there may be trespassing into each other's territory and duplication of work.

There should be clear structure for an organisation whose people have clear functions. Each level needs an understanding of what it is there to do and should then concentrate on that role. The aim of the flatter organisation is to have fewer levels, not the same number of levels crushed together.

We should also try to identify in each organisation and in each unit within it, clear functions both horizontally and vertically. The larger the space that each individual occupies the more room they have to grow. If, however, the space grows too big then there is a danger of the individual getting lost. Getting this right is a question of balance; most organisations err on the side of giving people too little personal space and whilst many of us have felt the restriction of corporate claustrophobia, rarely do we feel the panic of agoraphobia – a fear that we will get lost exploring the wide open spaces of our organisation.

How the structure finally ends up depends on the market, the technology and the product or service of the organisation. It depends on decisions about decentralisation and about the span of control required by the organisation. The span of control becomes an important mechanism in the clarifying of function and it is a way of ensuring that people do the job we want them to do. Give a supervisor a span of control of six and they can interfere regularly in the work of their staff; widen that span of control to twenty-five and the supervisor cannot help but stand back and manage performance strategically. Give a board of directors wider spans of control and they are forced to concentrate on their director duties and prevented from doing the work of their subordinates.

When we feel under pressure, most organisations are tempted to create assistants, deputies and intervening levels to coordinate and liaise. This is almost always a flawed response. The key task when working under pressure is to examine the activities and discard those that are no longer adding value; it is also the time to delegate work to others. Increasing numbers and levels as a short-term expedient always creates more long-term problems. Examine today's bureaucracies – everyone is busy, the creation of every job may have been supported by a well argued business case and the people are performing as well as they can. The end result is cluttered organisations spending more and more time on maintenance activities. They have been driven by *efficiency* – doing things right – rather than by *effectiveness* – doing the right things.

Reporting lines

One of the main principles which supported the old-style pyramidal organisation was that of 'Unity of Command' – everyone having one boss from whom they received clear and, hopefully, unambiguous instructions. In the modern organisation, unity of command has been sacrificed as the business world has become more complex.

People are now more likely to have several reporting lines, one of which may actually be their 'line manager'. This applies particularly to those organisations which have structured in a matrix or decentralised format. There are several working relationships that develop in an organisation:

- There is still the basic boss/subordinate relationship in which someone sets the priorities of subordinates and reviews their performance.
- Many people have a functional relationship (or 'dotted-line') with someone who gives them guidance/advice/coaching in a particular set of functional skills. For example, a multiple food retailer places its fresh food specialists under the local area manager, who appraises

them and sets their operational priorities. However, because the line manager does not have sufficient technical understanding of their specialism, they have a functional relationship with a fresh food director at head office who clarifies technical standards and manages their professional development.

- Project management involves some clear relationships between the project manager and the members of the project team.
- Many managers have a customer:supplier relationship in which they are required to respond to the needs of an internal customer department. If an employee has a line boss, as well as a function boss, sits on two project teams and has to provide a service to several parts of the organisation, clearly they have a web of reporting relationships to work out. The individual needs to know what authority relationships they have, in other words, who can ask them to do what. The situation is often complicated by two of those parties in the relationship having sharply contrasting views on a particular issue. When the line manager wants to 'ship more product' and the functional manager is carrying out a drive towards increased product quality, then the person in the middle begins to feel like a wishbone about to be pulled.

How do we manage this range of authority relationships?

1. The organisation, by simplifying its structure, may reduce its complexity, and consequently the need to develop too many authority relationships.
2. Clarify the precise nature of the relationship so that all parties understand their accountabilities. In a 'dual influence' situation such as the one shown in Figure 19, the factory manager and the divisional quality assurance manager will need to clarify responsibilities for the following:

   - How will the performance contract be drawn up?
   - Who will set performance standards?
   - Who will set day-to-day priorities?
   - What is the nature of the influence of the 'functional' manager (The Divisional quality assurance manager) on the work of the Quality assurance manager?
   - How will conflicts of interest be resolved?
   - Who is responsible for the individual's personal and career development?

They also need to agree their strategy on issues which affect the Quality assurance manager – no amount of structural work will overcome the conflict derived from major strategic differences.

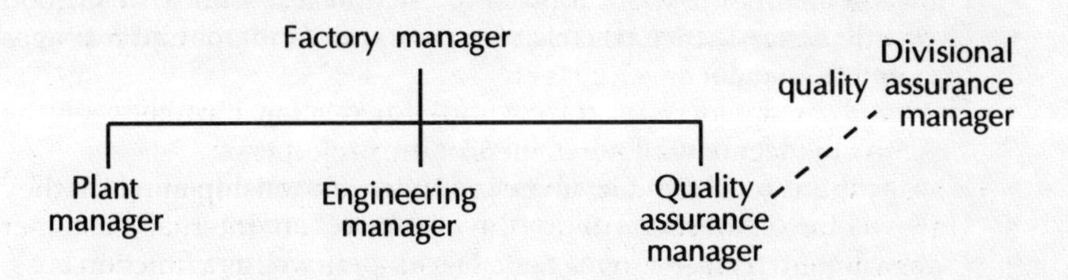

Figure 19 *Dual reporting lines*

3. The performance contracting process needs to take into account the whole network of relationships, so that the individual understands the whole range of performance requirements. This still places the line manager in the key authority relationship to the individual and puts an important responsibility on them to reflect the performance requirements of those other relationship managers.
4. Individuals who are in the middle of a web of authority relationships need to be trained to operate within those relationships. This involves developing the ability to manage ambiguity and to synthesise apparently conflicting priorities.

The key activity for managers must be to tackle these relationships 'up front' as it were. Time spent in defining reporting lines is much more positive than spending time disentangling them.

Decision making and implementing

Organisations need to clarify their *modus operandi* – literally their way of working. Establishing a structure and reporting lines is part of this process but other issues need to be addressed.

- How will new initiatives be agreed and integrated into the organisation?
- How will the work of different departments be coordinated?
- How will people get to know what is happening in other parts of the organisation?
- How are differences resolved within the organisation – between individuals, departments and functions?
- How, if people are encouraged to take initiative for their work, can that be directed towards the corporate goals?

- How far will the organisation go towards empowering employees to work in their own way?
- How will the organisation respond to external pressures to change?
- How will the organisation sense the external environment to identify the need to change?
- How will the organisation review and, if necessary, change its own structure to meet new requirements?
- How will the organisation develop effective internal relationships?
- How will the organisation allocate available resources?
- How will the organisation manage its own performance?

All these issues need to be clarified, effectively in one large performance contract, as a relationship building rather than as a conflict resolution activity. They need to be carried out for every organisation and in every part of the organisation – individual teams are after all, literally, a microcosm of the whole organisation with the same needs for internal processes and external sensitivity.

In my experience two sorts of issue arise within organisations in relation to their *modus operandi*. Firstly, large bureaucracies normally have clear procedures for introducing new initiatives but have a low level of responsiveness to external change; secondly, decentralised organisations are highly responsive to change but often lack the mechanisms for coordinating them across the whole organisation. Organisations today have to respond to change as well as having mechanisms in place to accommodate to those changes.

Accountability and authority

The final clarification exercise, which stems from the others, is that of clarifying individual accountability and authority: what is expected of the individual and what authority they will be given to enable them to achieve their accountabilities. This brings us back to the performance contract and the clarification of the performance and support requirements.

The important issue is that accountability should be matched by the appropriate level of authority. The job description, a much maligned document, should be used to settle both issues. The document should be a dynamic one – adding new activities and discarding redundant or non-essential work.

There are two key principles in the design of jobs which I want to relate to the issues of accountability and authority – leverage and headroom. The job needs to give individuals both the opportunity to influence things (leverage) and the space to grow and develop (headroom). This is where the concepts of accountability (leverage) and authority (headroom) need to be clarified so that people at work are carrying out a job which stretches them and gives them an area of autonomy in which they can operate. Several studies have shown that people work at their best when the following dimensions are present:

- The opportunity to develop new competence.
- Autonomy – responsibility for a discrete work area.
- Feedback on performance.
- The meaningfulness of work.

These factors are a combination of a good organisation structure and effective performance management. Job design, where people have influence and scope to develop brings the two factors together, along with an organisation structure which facilitates changes and helps rather than hinders the implementation of the business strategy.

14

Reward, Recruitment and Retention

The next set of 'Re' factors that we will look at need to be bracketed together – Recruitment, Retention and Reward. These concepts perform an important central role in creating a high performance environment because:

- they attract high performing people to the organisation;
- they help to retain those people within the organisation;
- they motivate them to perform as effectively as possible while they are there.

There are three important sets of needs within an organisation in relation to the three 'Re's'. Two of them relate to the people within the organisation, the third to the organisation itself.

We have a workforce that is made up increasingly of effective knowledge workers who have the potential to make significant changes to the organisations in which they work. These people working in information technology, marketing or personnel management are at the frontiers of change and not only have considerable skill and knowledge but are able to operate in turbulent market environments. Consequently they are very highly prized and valuable commodities. These people have high aspirations for their career and financial reward, they are well educated and require to be treated as individuals. This quite often goes against the collective focus of many large organisations whose remuneration and benefit strategies are still based on equity driven job-evaluation programmes. The American sociologist AW Gouldner has identified these people as 'cosmopolitans', key people whose loyalty is to their profession and to their own career development (see 'Cosmopolitans and locals: towards an analysis of latent social roles' in *Administrative Science Quarter*, 1957). He contrasted these with 'locals' – people with loyalty mainly to their organisation and who tend to have a career path which is mainly 'cradle to grave'.

RECRUITMENT AND RETENTION

The trick which organisations need to play is to attract and retain cosmopolitans whilst also retaining and motivating the locals. People who have a long and detailed knowledge of the organisation are valuable, but so are the people who come in and provide significant leadership over a short period of time before moving on to another professional challenge. Think back to the concept of performance contracting. As well as a performance contract between individual and manager, there also exists a psychological contract. This is between the organisation and the individuals within it, and must take into account the needs of both groups of people.

The local is more likely to be looking for security and stability, whilst also wanting job satisfaction and a stable career progression. The cosmopolitan is, however, more likely to be looking for a contract which provides the opportunity for professional growth and the opportunity to make high profile interventions in organisations in a stimulating way. They are likely to have a low tolerance of bureaucracy and to be relatively unconcerned with stability because of their habit of moving from job to job.

It is important to review in more detail the needs and expectations of cosmopolitans and locals. If we start to assume that all employees have the same needs and are motivated by the same thing then we are using the shotgun approach to reward and motivation – some of our benefits and policies will be an effective motivator and hit the target; other elements will miss the target altogether and their motivational effect will be diminished. Like the very old saying about advertising, 50 per cent of our rewards package may not be effective; the problem is working out *which* 50 per cent. We will examine this in more detail later in the chapter.

The difference between cosmopolitans and locals is an interesting dichotomy which exemplifies the problem of the modern remuneration and benefits director in developing a package which suits everyone whilst still gaining an appropriate return in terms of productivity. The cosmopolitan/locals analysis shows how people with different motivation operate within an organisation (Table 8).

Table 8 *Motivating factors in an organisation*

Cosmopolitans	Locals
• Look for a series of short, high profile assignments	• Look for a long and satisfying career
• Look for high reward for high risk activities	• Look for a reasonable reward for a job well done
• Are valued for their specialised knowledge and their track record	• Are valued for their experience within their organisation and their loyalty
• Are brought in to do a particular job with clear and stretching outcomes	• Work in whatever areas the company asks them to work
• Will probably make waves by introducing significant changes	• Work away at gradual and constant achievement
• Would leave the company for a better offer	• Would only leave the company at retirement or redundancy
• Are trained in prestigious business schools	• Are more likely to be trained in-company
• Give no thought for the morrow	• Want security and a good pension at the end
• Will leave the company if frustrated	• Will soldier on if frustrated but become tired and demotivated
• Work long hours in the day but want long holidays to recharge the batteries	• Prefer to work regular hours and take two weeks holiday at a time
• Accept that a large proportion of salary will fluctuate depending on performance	• Prefer a regular and dependable income
• Strive for public recognition and growth of professional reputation	• Operate quietly – prefer the respect of boss, peers and staff

This gives some measure of the dilemma facing personnel policy makers in relation to setting up human resource packages which appeal to both these two groups. My apologies to all readers if they feel that I have painted the local as a dull, pedestrian wage slave and the cosmopolitan as a flighty mercenary, ready to run off elsewhere at the siren call of the headhunter. Whilst these two extremes do exist, most people can be placed on a continuum between the two extremes.

The important factor in the analysis between 'cosmopolitans' and 'locals' is that there is an increasing trend in people to want to be recognised as individuals and this trend is seen particularly in the need for particular benefits. It is important for organisations to recognise that not everyone is a 'cradle to grave' employee with the same level of motivation and the same life style. Our benefits packages need to reflect the disparity of the workforce and, if they are to succeed as a motivator, those additional benefits should be applied to individuals in a way which is relevant and appropriate to their particular situation. Young people coming into an organisation have quite different requirements from women returners or from people nearing retirement and if the reward package is to give an appropriate incentive to everyone then it needs to be individually designed, however big a headache that may give to personnel administrators.

FLEXIBLE CONTRACTS

The subcontracting society which has been recognised by writers like Charles Handy and Alvin Toffler has already been mentioned. Organisations no longer need to keep everyone as full time, permanent employees and, in fact, there is a lot to be gained from subcontracting certain functions within an organisation to transfer them from a fixed cost base to a variable cost. To relate this to 'cosmopolitan' and 'local' dichotomy, the locals will be the established core of the organisation while the cosmopolitans take the jobs in the subcontractual fringe with high risk and high rewards.

Flexibility in both contract and benefits will attract a wide range of people who currently are not attracted by permanent full time employment and there are many people who may feel that their own personal performance is enhanced by a portfolio of roles within their life. Flexibility can be introduced in a number of areas:

1. Contracts need not be permanent and the introduction of fixed term contracts is an important mechanism to attract cosmopolitans who regard their career as a series of assignments, rather than a total commitment to one organisation. People who accept fixed term contracts are unlikely to want the full panoply of pensions, private health insurance and company cars, which are now an integral part of the senior benefits package. A simple fixed term contract dispensing with some of the peripheral benefits can add far more salary to the package and, therefore, become much more attractive to people who are motivated by the need for clear assignment targets and relatively high pay. Many cosmopolitans prefer to make their own arrangements for fringe benefits, which may neither attract nor motivate them in an employment contract.

2. The introduction of cafeteria benefits is another solution to attract and motivate the individual. Personnel systems are now becoming sufficiently flexible to make this a possible feature of most organisations' benefit packages in the future. Cafeteria benefit systems, whereby each benefit has a price and can be added up to make an attractive individual package, make the initial package more attractive to new recruits. It also retains people because they have the flexibility to change their package as their needs change and it creates a package which rewards and provides an appropriate incentive rather than giving people benefits which they don't value strongly but which nevertheless are an additional labour cost to the organisation. Cafeteria benefits packages have the capacity to create more 'motivation per pound' if they are effectively targeted.
3. By creating totally flexible benefits packages and contracts which enable people to work when they want to, everyone is treated as an individual which is, in itself, motivating.

It is quite important to ensure that there is some clear criteria on the price of each benefit so that certain people don't feel that they are being undervalued. A further advantage of an individual package is that it removes some of the status barriers in the organisation which can be so detrimental to morale and, subsequently, performance. When I first went into personnel management it was ironic that the young woman starting as a receptionist at 18 would often be put on the company's pension fund before her father who had thirty to forty years of blue collar service in the organisation. These sort of inequities have slowly been erased. However, there are still step changes in the benefit package, often quite arbitrary ones, at certain grade levels within an organisation. The harmonisation of terms and conditions of employment is an important goal for organisations without losing the option of rewarding people in pure salary terms for performance or increasing the range of benefits to which they become entitled.

The flexible packages for contracts, hours and benefits not only help to attract and retain; they must also be a way of meeting the organisation's needs for constantly increasing performance.

PERFORMANCE RELATED PAY

The next key remuneration issue is to relate payment closely to performance – so that people who perform well get higher pay without necessarily creating distortions in internal differentials within the organisation. Remuneration specialists have, in the past, seemed to aim towards paying everyone the same salary increase. There has been a significant regression to the mean in most organisations where managers have comfortably paid out 'normal' increases, whilst being very uneasy about paying increases at either the top or bottom end of the scale. The effect of this has been clear – retention of average people without offering them an incentive to develop and loss of high performers who have left in search of better remuneration packages elsewhere.

At a macro-level, some readers may recall the so-called 'brain-drain' in the sixties and seventies when this pattern was enacted at a national level and many of our key industrialists, academics, doctors, actors and pop stars fled the United Kingdom to avoid the high marginal tax rates which acted as such a huge disincentive to earn anything more than the average. Paying for performance is an important way forward for the future although according to the IPM/IMS survey, (see page 32) it has yet to be proven as an effective mechanism for delivering improved business performance. The problem is not necessarily the concept of paying for performance, but its application within large organisations.

It is important, where possible, to tie remuneration and benefits to performance or, at least, to ensure that the benefits package supports the organisational objectives. In my experience, too many organisations offer benefits which are service-related rather than performance-related. This is particularly noticeable in relation to the low mortgage facility which banks give on recruitment or on reaching a particular length of service. This service-related benefit, whilst effective in attracting and retaining staff, fails to meet the organisational needs for high performance. For the organisation to give a benefit after, say, two years service without any performance criteria attached gives a clear signal that turning up and doing your job is more important than achieving results and working towards the organisation's goals. It would be quite simple to give greater focus to such a benefit by linking it to the fulfilment of the performance contract.

We need to be very careful about the way we spend our manpower budgets. It is a matter of conventional wisdom that paying peanuts gets you monkeys. It is also true that it is more effective to attract a small cadre of highly skilled, highly paid people rather than a large team of moderately skilled, moderately paid people. Our remuneration and benefits package has a two-fold purpose. It is there to attract and retain, but it is also there to provide both incentive and reward for high performance. These two features need to be kept in mind during any discussion of remuneration.

A further objective of our reward strategy should be kept in mind. Our payment structure has a critical impact on the way people behave in an organisation. It is therefore an important lubricant for change and an important factor in creating new conditions. At one time, in personnel management, it was very unfashionable to believe that money was a motivator. I now believe that it was based on a rumour put about by personnel managers who wanted to keep the organisation within its wage budget! There can be no doubt that money has a motivational effect and that all other things being equal it can support technological and managerial change more effectively than almost anything else. A recent example of this has been the change in the relative use of leaded and unleaded petrol, before and after the differential petrol tax was introduced. More people began to use unleaded petrol when it became cheaper, having made the calculation that it was more beneficial to change the car over to unleaded petrol and pay for cheaper petrol in the future. Before that many people thought that it was a good thing to do but until it became an economically viable thing to do the change was not put into effect to the same level. This is very similar to how people regard work performance. They want to perform better but somehow it doesn't quite happen until there is a clear financial incentive to do so.

Performance related pay can have a very important effect on the direction of effort. The important thing is for organisations to clarify the level of performance that they require and then ensure that their pay systems support it. For example, wanting to reduce levels of management in an organisation can be effected by a well designed performance related pay structure, even if it is only a question of putting some of the cash saved by the reduction in levels into performance related pay for the people who remain. Conversely, there are many examples of organisations who have tried to reduce manpower levels whilst retaining job evaluation programmes which give more points for staff resources. This is an important example of the dissonance which is created when the organisation says one thing but continues to pay for another. Performance related pay and a performance management culture need to be coordinated and to work together. Without any mechanism for measuring and reviewing performance, the introduction of performance related pay is potentially disastrous and a business can be destroyed as the heat generated through angry debates between managers and subordinates about the nature of their bonus, burns up the whole organisation.

There are several things which an organisation needs to take into account if its performance pay structure is to support a performance management process.

Broad-based performance The organisation should be paying for performance across the whole job not just for certain key parts of the job. Performance pay structures based on one or two key outcomes which focus on, for example, sales or profit, often results in standards slipping in other areas as people try to maximise their income.

Recognition of both individual and team effort Payment for performance should, where possible, have elements which encourage effective individual performance and elements which encourage overall team performance. Many good working teams have been damaged by a performance related pay process which encourages the selfish achievement of individual objectives at the expense of others. Balancing the achievement of personal objectives against the achievement of team, SBU or company objectives can reinforce and enhance teamwork and become a mechanism to develop the organisation.

Unbiased reward schemes Performance payment schemes should have some element to encourage the whole organisation. Selective bonus schemes in which certain categories of staff (possibly sales or production) are incentivised whilst others remain on a basic pay system, create discord within the organisation and work against the creation of good working relationships. They also send clear messages to everyone about perceptions of importance within the organisation.

Competence incentives It may also be valid to pay for competence, particularly at lower levels in the organisation. In an organisation which is looking to increase multi-skilling, for example, additional payment for people who have learned new skills is an immediate incentive. At the lower levels in the organisation many people may need some form of monetary incentive to encourage them to take risks and move into areas which will require them to learn new skills. It is important, however, that the move to multi-skilling generates more benefits than the amount paid out to encourage the development of those skills.

Reflection of corporate objectives It is important to re-emphasise that pay, if it is to be an effective support to performance management, must reflect the corporate direction and must be used to support the organisation's objectives. There must be a clear idea of where the organisation is going and then the performance pay process can be used to help it get there.

There are two key concepts which need to be reviewed in the design of a performance pay programme. The first of these is *scope* – the potential for improving performance by the organisation or the individual or the team. It is impractical to set a programme in an area where little more real improvement can be effected. The second concept is *leverage* – the capacity of the individual or team to really influence business performance. For each performance pay system the individual or the team need to be clear about the targets which they have been set; the performance bonus needs to be based on things that the individual can influence and, if possible, it needs to be measurable by the individuals themselves so that there is little doubt about the amount of bonus or the amount of performance related pay that the individual or team will accrue. Excessively complicated schemes lose more goodwill in dysfunctional argument than they generate in improved productivity.

There are now a whole range of performance pay programmes in operation. An important one which relates to the theme of this book is to pay on the basis of achievement of a performance contract – quite simply, pay is based on the achievement of the key objectives in the contract. This particular system has the advantages of simplicity (either you achieve, exceed or fail to achieve); the payment supports the process of performance contracting, and the process covers the whole job – not just selected outcomes.

In a performance contract programme introduced by a major clearing bank there are three possible outcomes from the contract – Exceeded Contract, Met Contract or Failed To Meet Contract. The outcome of the contract affects two variables – the amount of performance bonus and the progression to salary maximum in a wide banded grading scheme which had been reduced from 21 grades to seven. This gave performance a key role in setting future salary levels and has had an important impact in changing the culture from activity to results orientation, and more importantly a results orientation that focused on meeting requirements across the whole job not just a few selected indicators.

Payment for performance, therefore, has an important impact on both the organisation's performance and on attracting and retaining people who can produce excellent results. A further advantage of performance related pay is its capacity for enhancing organisational performance at relatively little cost. A strategy of paying for performance ensures that money spent on remuneration has some measurable return and a well-designed scheme should be self-financing. It is the only alternative in times of recession where an increase in unit costs only leads to further business problems; performance related pay *can* lead the way out to business success.

Before setting out on a path towards performance related reward strategy, the organisation has to answer some important questions in relation to a wide range of issues:

The employment market

- What market am I in?
- How easy/difficult is it to recruit people?
- What do my key competitors pay?

- What is the total remuneration package within my market?
- Where do I want to be in relation to my competitors?

The organisation's mission

- What performance/capability do I want?
- What behaviours/attitudes do I want to encourage?
- How measurable are my performance requirements?
- How responsive are information systems? Can personal performance be tracked by the individual?

Remuneration policy

- How do I value internal equity?
- What are the key differentials in my business?
- What return do I require from my remuneration budget?
- What proportion of remuneration do I want to give over to reward/ incentivising performance?

Job design

- How much scope do individuals have to improve their job performance?
- What are the key factors which people within the organisation can influence?
- How closely do people need to work together to achieve the corporate mission?

The answers to these questions need to be reviewed before starting up a performance related pay programme.

The criteria for PRP schemes

There are several types of schemes and the remuneration analyst needs to consider some of the following options.

Individual, team or corporate focus? Performance pay can apply at all levels within an organisation. The key criteria for making the decisions are the amount of interaction between people and teams within the organisation. A high level of interaction or interdependence would be supported by schemes with a team or corporate base. The definition of performance requirements at individual, team and corporate levels is also key, particularly the need to differentiate between individual contributions.

Individual programmes can be paid as one-off bonuses or as merit based increments to base pay. One-off bonuses tend to be paid on the basis of achievement of key outcomes (sales, profit etc) whereas merit pay has, typically, been applied to performance across the whole job over a long period of time. Individual programmes are effective when there is a clear set of accountabilities with scope to improve performance through the efforts of the individual. The major disadvantage with individually focused programmes is that they may encourage the selfish pursuit of individual goals at the expense of others within the unit – thus individual payments are usually successful in a sales environment with mutually exclusive territories; they can be less helpful in a team of process operators.

Team bonuses are helpful in reinforcing the mutuality of people within a business. They need to be organised carefully – team performance can be enhanced by a well-designed individual scheme (one which has a set of individual goals which are geared to supporting other members of the team). The key to the success of team bonuses is the subtle and unremitting pressure of manager and peers to improve individual performance.

Corporate bonuses, in cash or shares, highlight the achievement of the corporate mission but are normally seen as too remote to have a major effect on the performance of individuals. They do, however, help to contain costs when the organisation's performance is poor.

Short or long-term? An important question for remuneration specialists is the balance of timing between short and long-term. Short-term measures tend to lead to short-term perspectives; long-term measures, whilst encouraging far-sightedness and business development, tend to be too far in the future to provide sufficient reward for present effort. The balance depends on the size and maturity of the organisation and the changing nature of the business environment and the market place. It also relates to the time horizon of the individual, which is normally, but not exclusively, a factor of seniority.

*Business Performance or competence?*The focus of most performance related pay programmes is normally some form of quantifiable business performance. Some organisations have encouraged the development of personal competence by designing a programme which pays for competence rather than job performance. It is arguable whether this is performance related or just an extension of the job evaluation process. It is, indirectly, a way of increasing performance and is most useful in jobs with a high technical content or in an environment where multi-skilling is seen as a key business incentive. An important caveat is that 'competence' or 'skill-based' schemes are potentially expensive if they are based on acquired competence rather than utilised competence (ie if an individual is paid to learn a skill which they use infrequently). A more cost-effective approach is to pay for new skills only when required – the organisation then gains the benefit of an enhanced skill base without inflationary pay policies.

*Reward or Incentive?*Incentives pay out automatically on the achievement of an agreed level of performance. Rewards are largely retrospective – paying for performance after it has been achieved. Incentives are normally seen as having a greater effect on behaviour because they state clearly what the individual or team will receive on the achievement of the desired behaviour. They are also potentially more expensive because they commit the company in advance to a specified level of expenditure, normally irrespective of the commercial situation which predominates at the time of the pay-out.

The choice between incentive and reward is not the most significant issue facing the remuneration professional. Most schemes operate on an incentive basis – whatever is chosen, the scheme needs to be based on clearly measurable outputs which are seen to have valid, desirable consequences on both individual and corporate performances.

*Outcome or whole job?*We have already reviewed this issue. Outcome (particularly single outcome) programmes based on sales or profit tend to be short-term and create problems when individuals distort short-term business performance in order to maximise their income, at the expense of sensible long-term strategies. This tendency can be mitigated by linking the bonus to 'whole job' issues such as the fulfilment or otherwise of the performance contract. This ensures that both output and capability measures are met and enables an organisation to strike a balance between, for example, production targets and product quality; customer attraction and customer retention; output and people development and so on.

These are all issues that must be considered before moving into performance related pay. Performance related pay is not, however, the only answer to motivation and the creation of a performance focused workforce. It can create the climate for performance but there is also a role for non-cash motivators in creating excellent performance.

MOTIVATION WITHOUT CASH

Many of these non-cash motivators are in the hands of the individual manager and if one were to characterise the two roles of the organisation and the manager in terms of individual motivation, it would be fair to say that in Herzberg's terms the organisation is responsible for ensuring that the hygiene factors are right, but only when the manager and the individual are fully committed can an environment be created in which the highest levels of performance are achieved.

Intrinsically, individuals motivate themselves. The manager can, however, enhance that motivation or put up barriers to prevent them working effectively. People at the very highest levels of motivation go beyond the motivating power of cash and benefits into something much greater – what Maslow, in *Motivation and Personality*, called self-actualisation. Principally the effective management of performance is to do with self-fulfilment. The manager can create an environment where the individual gains full motivation from their work:

- He or she can continually improve the work that an individual does and continually develop their skills and knowledge.
- He/she can clarify the job that the individual is expected to do, and make that job more satisfying by giving as much authority to the individual as is feasible. He/she can also make that job more interesting by expanding it slowly and delegating as much of his own work to the individual as possible.
- The manager can set targets for the individual and spell out the standards of work that are required.
- By providing accurate and well presented feedback, carrying out regular performance reviews and carrying out development discussions the manager can demonstrate where the individual is growing and developing and can increase the level of their contribution to the organisation as a whole.
- By encouraging individuals to work together as an effective team, the manager can create an environment where the synergy between individuals develops a level of collective performance which is much greater than the sum of the individuals.
- The manager can help to motivate an individual by trying to ensure that working conditions are conducive to effective work.

There are other factors which the organisation can provide which enhance the motivation of the individual. One barrier to motivation is that organisations are fundamentally inanimate and it is hard for people to respond enthusiastically to an inanimate object. Organisations do, however, develop strong cultures in which they can appeal to their employees as human beings. As a management consultant it is very difficult to identify why some organisations motivate people better than others, or rather why people in some organisations appear to be more highly committed than in others. The following points can be used as a check list to help you build up a picture of the performance of your own organisation.

- Support for employees during difficult times in their life – maternity leave, paternity leave, sickness leave.
- Positive support for people who are returning to work after a long period, particularly women returning from maternity leave.
- Good induction programmes which actively welcome people into the organisation and are extended by effective training programmes throughout the individual's career.
- Equal opportunities. Organisations who not only have a policy on equal opportunities, but who actively work to ensure that all groups are treated equally in terms of promotion, development and training.
- Effective communications in which the mission of the organisation is communicated enthusiastically to staff. An effective communications policy can greatly enhance commitment to a large organisation. It has always been recognised that large organisations have greater problems in relation to the management of people than small businesses where people are more likely to feel that they know what's going on and are listened to. This can be enhanced by processes such as team briefing, internal communications programmes and quality circles.
- Career development across the organisation, particularly where vacancies are fairly filled by open systems. Open internal recruitment systems can be unpopular with managers who often have a very clear idea who they want to take up a particular position. However, the feeling that vacancies are being filled behind closed doors creates ill-feeling within an organisation in that however hard one may try the race is not always won by the fastest person. This has a depressing effect on individual motivation.
- Complete openness with staff is critical: this should be encouraged by top management and further enhanced by managers throughout the organisation. It is important to treat people as adults and in my experience if we do so they are likely to behave as adults, contributing wholeheartedly to the achievement of the organisation's objectives and participating as equal members of the enterprise, rather than simply as hands in a faceless bureaucracy or as potentially delinquent schoolchildren.

Recruitment, retention and reward policies are critically important issues to get right if they are to attract and keep the right people and to motivate people when they are at work. This strategic alignment of human resource processes is a critical support to the effective operation of performance management processes within the organisation. If there is no strategic alignment the organisation confuses its people by sending out a wide range of contradictory messages about performance and motivation; if there is a strategic alignment of policies and processes reinforcing each other, it has a powerful multiplier effect on the important themes supporting the organisation's mission.

CREATING THE ORGANISATION'S BRAND AS AN EMPLOYER

This process is similar to the process of creating a brand in product marketing. Truly successful brands develop a series of complementary characteristics over a period of time. Not every product becomes a brand; many stay as rather dull, disparate products whereas the effective brand endures and continues to build its reputation. A brand is a set of perceptions in the mind of the consumer, in the same way an organisational culture is a set of perceptions in the mind of the employee, or the potential employee.

Why do people want to work for Marks and Spencer, IBM and ICI? Because the messages that their customers and employees transmit say that the organisation is a good place to work and that the culture is progressive. Organisational identities are not made by the clever copywriting of an advertising agency; they are developed over a long period by the constant positive reinforcement of the organisation's values.

Departmental cultures also exist – certain parts of an organisation give off an air of enthusiasm and excitement; they have credibility – that most evanescent of features – and they are places where people really want to work.

The branding of organisations starts when they regard it as important to offer as clear a proposition to their employees as they do to their customers. Again, this is more than creating a glossy image as a recruiter – it is as important to clarify the brand in the minds of existing employees as in the perceptions of potential employees. One of the most important features of an effective brand is the way that it is communicated to other people. Communication is a necessary, but not a sufficient condition of an effective brand. There has to be some genuine substance to communicate, otherwise the glossy ads are nothing more than a slick public relations exercise. However, failure to communicate represents an important lost opportunity in relation to motivation, retention and recruitment. One of the most important ways to communicate the organisation's brand is by the recruitment process.

THE RECRUITMENT PROCESS

In the same way as warfare is too important to leave to the generals, so recruitment is too important to leave to the recruiters. Recruitment decisions should not be delegated by the line manager although they should be supported by the expertise of a professional recruiter. Recruitment is an important investment decision for the organisation because it is a large investment, much greater than most of the capital decisions that an organisation will make. If we add salaries, on-costs, office accommodation and secretarial support even a middle manager in an organisation can cost up to £100,000 per year – a significant investment especially when viewed in the long term, with salaries increasing at, say, 10 per cent per annum over a period of ten years. To delegate recruitment decisions of this magnitude to the personnel manager and a battery of psychometric tests is almost criminal negligence on the part of the organisation. However competent the personnel manager may be, the line manager must be fully involved.

From the manager's point of view, the recruitment of a new individual means making an adjustment to the constitution of the team. To recruit somebody with high potential who fits well into the existing work team is a huge asset and is likely to enhance considerably the work of the team. However, to recruit somebody, however competent, who doesn't work well with the other members of the team and does not fit in to the performance culture of the organisation is not only an expensive mistake in itself; it may also damage the previously effective working performance of the team.

Introducing a new manager into an organisation is never a neutral event; it either adds or subtracts value. The first component of effective selection is the amount of time taken by senior executives in the recruitment of their staff. We should spend a lot of time carrying out recruitment exercises because they are far-reaching in their consequences. It is also important for the potential recruit that we should spend time bringing them on board. The selection process is a two-way decision making process – the organisation makes a decision about the individual and the individual makes their decision about the organisation. Decisions of this magnitude for both parties are enhanced by the collation of information which can only be gathered through a number of face to face meetings. For both parties it is the small details about the individual and the organisation which give the more accurate picture. It is important that we move the selection process away from the corporate public relations image, supported by those glossy brochures and flashy presentations which always promote suspicion that the organisation is on its best behaviour for the duration of the selection process.

Both parties need time to make their judgements and that time needs to be made available. It is ironic that many managers in organisations spend less time recruiting their people than they would selecting a piece of equipment. There are far more issues involved in recruitment than simply making a decision based on a CV, a psychometric profile and a one hour unstructured interview.

It is important to state the requirements of the job at an early stage so that recruitment time is spent on the few key applicants who meet those requirements. If there are only five or six applicants for a key job, this can be successful provided that one of those meets specification exactly. Many of the problems created by selection procedures stem from the lack of clarity of the job function and person that is required. We need to develop a clear idea of the sort of person that our organisation requires and communicate that clearly in our recruitment advertising in order to discourage unsuitable applicants – this is an important part of our branding process. By doing this we can ensure that unsuitable people select themselves out of the job, leaving us with a cluster of people who are genuinely suitable and who we should then work with closely to ensure that we finally recruit the most suitable. We are also in a stronger position to provide them with information about the company in more depth and with more frankness rather then expecting them to rely on the glossy brochure filled with pictures of high tech offices and pen pictures of smiling recent recruits with their 'spontaneous' comments about the organisation (which have been carefully drafted by a team of public relations specialists).

Attracting high performers

We must try to sell our organisation to the people who we want to join us, but to sell the organisation on the basis of its track record, the challenging environment in which it operates and the size of the job that we want people to do. By attracting people who want to give high performance, we add value to the organisation and create a stimulus for other people inside the company to stretch themselves to perform better.

Our interviewing style should also be directed to identifying people who will work effectively in a high performance culture. This will mean more careful structuring of interviews and a more direct focus on recent demonstrable past performance rather than vague questions about hypothetical future performance. The interview must be a process of deriving information about past performance in order to make judgements about future potential within our organisation. Well constructed, challenging interviews generate important evidence about the individual whilst giving a clear message to them that the organisation that they are applying to join is one in which high performance is a pre-condition of employment and that the interviewer is not looking for social poise and membership of the right clubs. The interview process is often lowly rated in terms of predictive validity but by focusing on key skills in the job and asking questions which are designed to extract information which relates to those criteria, the interview can become far more valid as an accurate predictor of future job performance.

The aim here is not to review the range of selection techniques such as psychometric testing, assessment centres and the assessment of biodata, but to ensure that, whatever selection techniques are used, those people recruited to the organisation are predisposed to higher performance. Understanding what makes your best performers tick is a key role of the personnel department and of the organisation as a whole. The people who are the leading edge of performance in your organisation are the people who need to be replicated. An organisation should look five to ten years ahead on a regular basis to try to identify the sort of people who are likely to be needed in the future; and to review the levels of skills and knowledge that they are likely to need.

Professionalism – the key to successful recruitment

The whole process of recruitment needs to reflect the professionalism of the organisation. Although it should be time intensive, it should not be drawn out or sloppy. The key is the creation of a brand image; an image that makes people *want* to work and perform within that organisation. The recognition of a successful brand is differentiation, standing out from the herd; creating a recruitment process which makes people want to join your organisation is an important part of that. Well-produced literature, letters promptly answered, a professional welcome and an opportunity to find out real facts about the company are all things which support and promote the brand – they do not create it. That can only be done by the development of a coherent set of performance management strategies, supporting a clear sense of commitment to a meaningful mission.

These issues – reward, recruitment and retention – create an important focus for the personnel or human resource function. The role of the human resource function is to create an environment in which the organisation attracts and retains high performers and stimulates them to perform and develop. It moves the personnel function towards added value activities and away from the maintenance type functions which have traditionally been their province.

To summarise, the need to set up appropriate organisational environments creates the need for the following policies:

1. A reward mechanism which encourages individual performance and directs it towards the achievement of corporate goals.
2. The creation of a clear organisational brand which differentiates the organisation as an employer and clarifies the psychological contract between the organisation and its employees.
3. Policies which attract, retain and motivate both cosmopolitans and locals.
4. Benefits which are as individually driven as possible and provide stimulus towards constantly improving business performance.
5. A careful and precise recruitment process which takes into account the needs of both recruiter and candidate.

15

Implementing Performance Management Programmes

It is important to end a book on performance management with a chapter on implementation. Corporate strategies and human resource consultants so often concentrate on the strategic concepts at the expense of the execution. Organisations see a package that they like and implement it as quickly as possible, frequently without thinking through some of the broader issues involved in its introduction.

Performance management involves a change in the culture and orientation of the organisation. It involves moving from activity to results; this requires measurement of performance and much more regular feedback than before. These issues, if not introduced in the right way, can be dysfunctional and will certainly be perceived as threatening. The implementation of an effective performance management process needs to be seen as an incremental change rather than a step change – a change in style and approach which gradually becomes embedded in the corporate *modus operandi* rather than a quick fix and a flashy package which is later replaced by another fix of some other hallucinatory substance which creates the illusion of progress rather than delivering the reality.

There are several important prerequisites for the successful implementation of a performance management process. These need to be carefully set in place if the process is to be effective. To implement a performance related pay process, for example, before the performance management process is in place is almost guaranteed to cause more problems than it resolves.

A responsive management information system

It is difficult to manage performance effectively without some clear measures of performance; the consequences of those measures cannot be adequately managed without a management information system (MIS) which gives good data on a regular basis. A simple system which takes some key measures for the business plan for each individual and ensures that they receive regular feedback on these measures is far more helpful, in my experience, than a complex process which fails to generate information quickly. Effective conglomerates such as GEC and Hanson, have long managed disparate businesses by clarifying the key measures which indicate the health of the business and giving regular feedback on these; thus both the manager and the managed are able to take action at an early stage.

A clear corporate mission

If the function of performance management is the delivery of the corporate mission, then the existence of a clear and unambiguous set of corporate objectives would seem to be a necessary precondition for effective performance management. We have already seen that an understanding of not only the business objectives but also the critical factors in the business that create success and the key business process behind those factors is the key to good performance management. Only when the business has a clear idea of its direction can it move ahead with programmes which are designed to help it move there more quickly.

A contractual management style

The organisation needs to have an open approach to management, one which recognises people as equals and enables clear and open communication. The management by command style does not translate effectively from an imposed management by objectives style to a more collaborative performance contract process. The organisation needs to clear the main barriers to performance – functional, bureaucratic, status and so on – out of the way before it can start to embark on an effective performance management process.

An understanding of competency

The organisation needs to understand what job competences people need to enable them to carry out their role effectively and those broader characteristics which make people successful within the organisation. Both of those areas need to be clearly linked to the business mission so that the organisation is developing its people capabilities to ensure future succession. A clear understanding of the business mission and the skills which are required to achieve it are critical to the successful attainment of those two aspects of the performance cycle – business performance and personal development.

A pro-active personnel function

The concept of performance management gives a sense of purpose and meaning to the personnel/human resource function. It moves away from the 'administrative-welfare' roles towards what Bevan and Thompson (see page 31) refer to as the 'strategic-facilitator' role. The issues of personnel strategy – manpower planning, reward/retention, recruitment, performance appraisal, management development and training are brought together into a strategically aligned and effectively coordinated programme designed to deliver the corporate mission, whilst enhancing personal and corporate development of capability. This involves a function which is:

- co-ordinated – producing a set of processes which are mutually reinforcing;
- commercial – delivering the business plan and taking key responsibility for enhancing human resource capability;
- influential – able to have an impact across the whole business on issues which are central to the performance and development of the business.

With these prerequisites in place, the organisation can move towards the development of a performance management culture, taking into account some of the following issues:

1. It is critical to paint the wide picture of the organisation's requirements for performance and how the organisation is likely to get there. The coordination of the whole process is important if key line managers are to understand the direction of performance management within the organisation and how it pervades all aspects of management.
2. The road to effective performance management needs to be incremental – a great leap forward in terms of sophistication and complexity may leave people within the organisation struggling to keep up, thus dissipating the beneficial elements of the performance management process.

   The first step is to decide what needs to be measured and start by measuring the status quo. Setting measures for each critical success factor is the first step. Once those measures have been validated (that is, confirming that they measure what they are intended to measure) then they can provide the basis for setting standards and targets across a unit or across the whole organisation.

3. When valid and reliable measures have been set up and are operating successfully – and when a clear set of competences have been clarified – the organisation is in a position to review the implementation of performance related pay and to set the basis of the scheme. Performance related pay programmes raise the temperature of performance management and need to be introduced into the organisation when measurement of performance and competence, as well as the skills of managers in that area, are sufficiently robust to enable pay rates to relate to the system.
4. Simple measures should be introduced at first. These can be improved and made more sophisticated as the capacity of information systems and the capability of managers to work with more complex measures increases.
5. A critical factor in the management of performance is the training and support of managers in performance management. One draw-back of some performance contracting processes is the open-ended nature of the process, coupled with a lack of training for its introduction. Managers need support initially in one of two ways, either extensive training in objective setting and guidance in review process, or a set of procedures which, initially at least, guide the manager through the process by giving a high level of direction on the nature of the performance objectives or competence analysis. This high level of direction can safely be diluted when managers and staff become more familiar with the process and develop more skill in the measurement and review of performance.

The key training issues are:

- setting effective performance measures;
- matching performance levels with an appropriate amount of management support;
- giving effective and timely feedback on performance;
- carrying out an effective performance review meeting;
- assessing performance against objectives;
- carrying out an effective development discussion;
- reviewing development of personal competence;
- participation in succession planning and potential assessment exercises.

Implementing performance management is critical if the organisation is to deliver its mission, both short- and long-term. The process is incremental – a gradual improvement and sophistication in both the measures themselves and the organisation's capability. Recent research shows that targeted programmes carefully implemented can have an effect in achieving company business targets; complex programmes rushed in without thought or preparation are unlikely to generate any enhanced business performance.

Selected Further Reading

The aim of this book has been to act as a guide to the various components of effective performance management. The following book-list should help any reader who wants to explore the subject further.

Blanchard, K, Zigarmi, P and Zigarmi, D (1985) *Leadership and the One Minute Manager* Fontana, London.

A more detailed review of 'contracting for leadership style' – a key part of the performance contract.

Covey, S (1989) *The Seven Habits of Highly Effective People* Simon and Schuster, New York and London.

An important description of how individuals can make themselves more effective.

Francis, D (1985) *Managing Your Own Career* Fontana, London.

A book about people taking charge of their own career development – a necessary condition of effective performance management.

Handy, C (1989) *The Age of Unreason* Hutchinson, London.

A book about the discontinuity of life in general in the 1990s with some particularly thought-provoking chapters on the structure of organisations in the future.

Hemery, D (1986) *Sporting Excellence* Collins Willow, London.

An interesting read about athletic performance and coaching skills with obvious parallels to life in modern organisations.

Herriot, P (1989) *Recruitment in the 90s* Institute of Personnel Management, London.

A concise and readable book about the importance of thoughtful selection.

Hersey, P and Blanchard, K (1989) *Management of Organisational Behaviour* Prentice Hall, New Jersey.

A comprehensive review of a wide range of issues relating to motivation, authority, leadership and behaviour. The academic basis of the more popular *One Minute Manager* series.

Khadem, R and Lorber, R (1986) *One Page Management* Quill, New York.

Describes the way in which the effective management of information can support the effective management of performance.

Mager, R F and Pipe, P (1990) *Analysing Performance Problems* Kogan Page, London.

A practical guide to the systematic analysis of the sins of omission and commission which happen when people fail to meet their performance contract.

Minzberg, H (1983) *Structuring in Fives – Designing Effective Organisations* Prentice Hall, New Jersey

A comprehensive review of structural issues in the modern organisation.

Moss Kanter, R (1989) *When Giants Learn to Dance* Simon and Schuster, New York and London.

A book which describes some of the structural and career implications of the changing business operations of the 1990s. It highlights the need to remain flexible and open to change.

Mumford, A (1989) *Management Development – Strategies for Action* Institute of Personnel Management, London.

An effective and practical approach to the formal and informal processes of developing managers and directors.

Naisbitt, J and Aburdene, P (1985) *Re-inventing the Corporation* Futura, London.

Along with the *Megatrends* series, this is a stimulating and imaginative review of the future and how it will affect the structure and operation of the modern organisation.

Neale, F (ed) (1991) *The Handbook of Performance Management* Institute of Personnel Management, London.

A series of chapters on the main elements of performance management based on case studies from a range of large organisations. The case studies demonstrate that different organisations come into performance management through a different door, as it were, but often end up in the same house.

Peters, T (1987) *Thriving on Chaos* MacMillan, London.

The most revolutionary of the Tom Peters series and written with his customary verve. Many managers find him a little too overstated and his prescriptions too revolutionary, but he is a great antidote to the dull, mechanistic management style.

Potter, B (1985) *The Way of the Ronin – Riding the Waves of Change at Work*, Ronin Publishing, Berkeley, California.

Ronin were 'freelance samuai' in Medieval Japan, responsible for managing their own development and finding their own work. Beverley Potter's book is a very perceptive and readable approach to maintaining and developing personal competence in an environment of change.

Porter, M (1985) *Competitive Advantage* Collier MacMillan, New York.

One of the best respected books on corporate strategy. Without a clear idea on strategy and the elements which give an organisation it's competitive edge, performance management processes are bound to be ineffective. A clear organisational strategy is a necessary but not sufficient condition of effective performance management.

Reddin, B (1988) *The Output Oriented Organisation*, Gower, Aldershot.

Bill Reddin has described how to create an organisation with an output focus – ie clarity on what the organisation and the people within it are there do to. This element of his book is particularly useful along with the descriptions of how this can be achieved.

Rowbottom, R and Billis, D *Organisation Design – The Work Levels Approach* Gower, Aldershot.

An important book on organisation design. The work levels approach is a rigorous way of examining the levels of an organisation to ensure that they add value.

Schumacher, E F (1973) *Small is Beautiful* Abacus, London.

A classic on the nature of work and the structure of organisations.

Stewart, Valerie and Andrew (1982) *Managing the Poor Performer* Wildwood House, Aldershot.

This deals with the important topic of managing poor performance in a positive and thoughtful way. It tackles some key issues in individual performance.

Terry P, (1984), *The Winning Mind* Thorson, Wellingborough.

An interesting book on the psychology of sporting performance – with many ideas to enhance that ephemeral characteristic – confidence.

Index